"Ask Dr. Dixie is a big hit with our newspaper readers! With over 100,000 readers each week, Dr. Dixie is reaching out with open arms to embrace readers with God's ability to heal and bring understanding and wisdom to life's challenges. I know readers will enjoy having so many of Dr. Dixie's columns in one book!"

—Phillip Reid, Reid Family Newspapers

Ask ✓
Dr. Dixie

Ask ✓
Dr. Dixie

NEWSPAPER READERS ASK THE CURIOUS
Questions about
GOD

Dr. Dixie Yoder

from the pages of Dr. Dixie's syndicated column

TATE PUBLISHING
AND ENTERPRISES, LLC

Ask Dr. Dixie
Copyright © 2013 by Dr. Dixie Yoder. All rights reserved.

No part of this publication may be reproduced, stored in a retrieval system or transmitted in any way by any means, electronic, mechanical, photocopy, recording or otherwise without the prior permission of the author except as provided by USA copyright law.

Scripture quotations marked (AMP) are taken from the *Amplified Bible*, Copyright © 1954, 1958, 1962, 1964, 1965, 1987 by The Lockman Foundation. Used by permission.

Scriptures marked as (CEV) are taken from the *Contemporary English Version*, Copyright © 1995 by American Bible Society. Used by permission.

Scripture quotations marked (HCSB) are taken from the *Holman Christian Standard Bible*®, Copyright © 1999, 2000, 2002, 2003 by Holman Bible Publishers. Used by permission. Holman Christian Standard Bible®, Holman CSB®, and HCSB® are federally registered trademarks of Holman Bible Publishers.

Scripture quotations marked (MSG) are taken from *The Message*. Copyright © 1993, 1994, 1995, 1996, 2000, 2001, 2002. Used by permission of NavPress Publishing Group.

Scripture quotations marked (NASB) are taken from the *New American Standard Bible*®, Copyright © 1960, 1962, 1963, 1968, 1971, 1972, 1973, 1975, 1977, 1995 by The Lockman Foundation. Used by permission.

Scripture quotations marked (NCV) are taken from the *New Century Version*®. Copyright © 2005 by Thomas Nelson, Inc. Used by permission. All rights reserved.

The opinions expressed by the author are not necessarily those of Tate Publishing, LLC.

Published by Tate Publishing & Enterprises, LLC
127 E. Trade Center Terrace | Mustang, Oklahoma 73064 USA
1.888.361.9473 | www.tatepublishing.com

Tate Publishing is committed to excellence in the publishing industry. The company reflects the philosophy established by the founders, based on Psalm 68:11,
"The Lord gave the word and great was the company of those who published it."

Book design copyright © 2013 by Tate Publishing, LLC. All rights reserved.
Cover design by Rtor Maghuyop
Interior design by Jake Muelle

Published in the United States of America
ISBN: 978-1-62295-717-0
Religion / General
12.12.26

Table of Contents

God Won't Give You More Than You Can Handle . . . 9
The Beaver Cleaver Myth. 13
Opportunities and Opposition 17
Is Transparency in Marriage Biblical?. 21
Why Get Married?. 27
Enablement Produces Disablement 33
Music Matters 37
Anger and Sunsets 41
The "Grizzly Bear" of Margin-less Living 45
Margin-less Living and Irritation. 49
Life Should Be Fun, Fair, and Free. 55
Information Overload and Intolerance. 59
The Sin of Self-Discipline 63
Eternal GPS: *God*'s Positioning System 67
Wanna Borrow a Jack? 73
Judge Not! Or Not? 77
The Birth of Rage. 83
The Solution for Rage 87
Adrenaline Junkies and Extreme Living. 91
Saving, Collecting, or Hoarding? 95
Thankful Giving Eliminates Hoarding. 99
Fall Back, Spring Forward 103
Choosing Peace Instead of Misery 107
Why Pain? 111
Jesus and Politics. 115

Choice: Blessing or Curse?	119
"Arithmetic" of Worry	123
What's Good About Good Friday?	127
"Average" Kate Changes History	131
From Commoner to Royalty	135
Why God Created People	141
"Daddy, My Daddy, Sir"	145
The Broken Gospel	149
Real Men	153
Real Women	161
Unisex is not a Third Gender	167
Does God Have A Favorite Gender?	173
Prejudice Is A Two-Way Street	177
Our Declaration of Dependence	181
Do You Sit in the Cellar or Perch on the Porch?	185
Tornadoes and Emotions—Twins?	189
God's Stimulus Package	195
Untwisting Twisted Thinking	199
I Can't Stop Thinking "I Can't"	203
The Lord Gives … and the Lord Takes Away?	207
Does God Take or Receive Our Loved Ones?	211
The End Is Near!	215
Mayans and the End of Time	219
The Birth of Jesus and the End of Time	223
Christmas Receiving	227
Atheism Says, "Jesus Is Not the Reason"	231
Jesus: The Reason We Celebrate	237
New Year's Resolutions	243

Dr. Dixie, people often say, "God won't give you more than you can handle." If God knows we're weak, why does He give us hard things to begin with?

—Overloaded

Dear Overloaded,

This statement is a misquotation of 1 Corinthians 10:13: "No trial has overtaken you that is not common to man. God is faithful, and will not allow you to be tested beyond what is possible to endure, but in the trial will provide *the way* of escape."

Misquoting this verse and taking it out of context wrongly communicates that we can only hope God will stop allowing difficulties to pile up on us when He realizes we're about to collapse, decreasing burdens at the last second so we won't cave in. But since we all know people who *have* collapsed under the pressure, there's really no assurance in the statement "God won't give us more than we can handle." So what does 1 Corinthians 10:13 mean?

We must remember that *God isn't the originator of hard things.* Sinful choices and the impact of original sin on God's entire creation produce difficult circumstances in life. Birth defects occur because genes and chromosomes are flawed and cannot produce

The ...
the trials of th...
journey. This contex...
word *peirasmos* should be ...
Paul says they failed the testing ...
they "passionately craved evil things" (Wu...
New Testament). They complained consta...
therefore, "God was not pleased with the great majority of them." God was at work in their journey to bring them to maturity and the fullness of the Promised Land. Their wrong response kept them in immaturity and lack.

Here are some practical truths to be gained from 1 Corinthians 10:1–13:

1. God is always trustworthy.
2. Satan uses hard times to tempt us to doubt God's faithfulness.
3. God uses the hard times as an opportunity for us to examine our responses and growth for the purpose of refinement and purification.

4. God will never leave His children alone in a test of any kind.
5. Every test has the potential for benefit and victory.
6. God deals with our *ability to withstand* the test.
7. We must deal with our *willingness to trust* God in the time of testing.

God promises to provide "a way to walk out" of each trial victoriously. Jesus *is the way*, the road, the means (John 14:6).

> "In the world you have tribulation, trials, distress and frustration; but be cheerful, confident ... undaunted! *I have deprived the world of power to harm you. I have conquered it for you!*"
>
> John 16:33b (AMP)

God knows far better than we do that we cannot "handle" anything on our own! But He guarantees His immediate and constant work in whatever situation we face. "Because God is a partner in their labor, *all things are fitting into a plan for good* for those who love God and are called according to His purpose" (Romans 8:28 AMP).

Write 1 Corinthians 10:13.

_____
_____
_____

Write Romans 8:28.

_____
_____
_____

What is "the way" out of trials?

_____
_____
_____

Ask the Lord to show you the three things He most wants you to know about Himself.

_____
_____
_____

Ask the Lord to show you the three things He most wants you to know about yourself.

_____
_____
_____

The Beaver Cleaver Myth

Dr. Dixie, we've just celebrated Mother's Day and Father's Day within an epidemic of "dysfunction." Really, since Ward, June, Wally, and Beaver Cleaver, has a *functional* family existed? If God is so wise, why couldn't He come up with a decent plan for relationships?

—Cynical About Families and God

Dear Cynical,

The family design emerges in Genesis 1–2 when God created the first man and woman, instructing them to "be fruitful and multiply." From the beginning, God intended to "grow" human families by sharing with us the privilege of co-creating with Him. Family is the organism that, functioning as God designed it, provides safety and nurture for helpless babies; it is a place to grow, love, and build together, encouraging each other's highest potential.

Current studies by social pundits, many of whom make no claim of knowing God, still show that God's original design is the right environment for "growing" healthy human beings. Research verifies beyond doubt that ample time spent enjoying family adds years to our lives and that quality family relationships contribute to overall lifelong well-being in much greater measure than financial plenty.

We experience our initial social interactions with family. When these interactions take place with emotionally steady adults who humbly and obediently love God, children develop a healthy perspective of themselves and others. Because our families—parents, siblings, grandparents, and extended family—nurture us in childhood while we're totally dependent, our perspective of what God is like comes predominately from them.

God's design for a complete family begins with a man and a woman who love God and are thoughtfully and carefully married in a lifelong commitment to each other. As they co-create with God, this male father and female mother carefully teach their children how to love God and other people with decreasing selfishness. When a complete family is damaged though death, extended family and a wise second marriage can be very beneficial to the process of continuing stable emotional growth in the children involved.

But when family systems repeatedly fail through selfish choices, the children's understanding of God's love and goodness is shattered. Satan's attack against family is vicious. He knows that the deep spiritual and emotional damage caused by broken families makes them far more vulnerable to his attack. Children who aren't deliberately and thoughtfully trained by maturing parents to reject selfishness grow up accepting the poison of entitlement as normal. This inevitably destroys the relationships they try to build.

Violence, divorce, unmarried sexual encounters, and repeated careless remarriages cause such deep emotional trauma that Biblically normal and stable relationships become impossible apart from a healing relationship with the Lord Jesus. Seventy-five percent of divorced people remarry—half within three years. Seventy-six percent of second marriages fail within five years; 87 percent of third marriages fail (allaboutfamilies.org). And the cycle continues into future generations.

This failure to thrive in families is not a reflection of God's lack of goodness and wisdom, but evidence of our rebellion against His gracious authority. We live in a "say yes to the dress" culture that considers how we're dressed for forty-five minutes to be more important than how we act for the next forty-five years. The Cleaver family wasn't perfect. But they exhibited commitment, respect for others, and determination to work through difficult things.

Until we choose to live obediently within God's protection, we'll increasingly experience the horrifying results of our own selfishness—sexual promiscuity, STDs, divorce, poverty produced by single-parent homes, and rebellious, bitter, enraged children. The mess in relationships is *our* doing, not God's. The solution is to know our Heavenly Father and to receive His love.

Write Titus 2:3–5.

_____
_____
_____
_____
_____

Write 1 Peter 3:7.

_____
_____
_____

Write Ephesians 6:1–3.

_____
_____
_____
_____
_____

Find three things that God specifically says about family, respect, and honor.

_____
_____
_____

Opportunities and Opposition

Dr. Dixie, people say, "when God closes a door, He opens a window." The implication seems to be that when God says okay to something, we won't have any struggle and that everything will "fall in place." Overall, that has not been my experience. Is it true that if something is "God's will," things will go smoothly?

—Opposed to Opposition

Dear Opposed,

The assumption that if we are "in God's will," then things will go smoothly cannot be supported by Scripture. Jesus is the prime example. He was perfectly obedient and carried out His life purpose exactly as He was instructed to do. Yet He faced constant opposition, rejection, and what appeared at the time to be an untimely death. We probably wouldn't describe that as a "smooth" life—certainly not trouble-free! But because Jesus was empowered by the love of God, His earthly life completely changed the direction of human existence. Instead of *preventing* Him from successfully completing His purpose, the opposition Jesus faced became the *vehicle* to His successful life, death, and resurrection.

The principle of aerodynamics illustrates how opposition is beneficial. Briefly explained, flight occurs when the power of the engine pushes the aircraft forward on the runway into the opposition of headwind. As increasing speed creates greater airflow, the shape of the wings *causes less air pressure to push down on the wings than is pushing up.* This difference in pressure creates lift, an upward force that overcomes the downward force of gravity. When the upward lift is greater than the downward gravitational force, the airplane flies. *Drag* is the friction created by a moving aircraft, constantly opposing its forward motion through the air. In order to remain in flight, the thrust of power must be greater than the drag, and upward lift must be greater than the downward force of gravity.

For the believer, every opportunity for advancement into spiritual maturity will be impeded by resistance. Satan, like the pressure of gravity, constantly opposes and assaults the spread of righteousness. Our ever-present flesh "drags down" our forward momentum into spiritual and emotional maturity. God is the enabling power that far surpasses any opposition we face. Because the "thrust" of His power is greater than the "drag" of opposition, "lift" is created that elevates us above the "gravitational" circumstances that seem bent on pulling us down. Resistance from people and circumstances isn't an *insurmountable hindrance to successful Christian living.* Rather, it's a force, like a strong headwind, that combines with our dependence upon the love-power of God and *lifts us beyond the control of difficult circumstances*, even if circumstances don't change.

> For my determined purpose is that I may know Him, that I may progressively become

> more deeply and intimately acquainted with Him ... and that I may in that same way come to know the power outflowing from His resurrection ... That if possible I may attain to the spiritual and moral resurrection *that lifts me out from among the dead even while in the body.*
>
> Philippians 3:10–11 (AMP)

The blind beggar Bartimaeus (Mark 10:46–52) didn't let the resistance of cultural disapproval stop him from attracting Jesus's attention. Ten leprous men ignored the opposition of societal fear, calling out to Jesus as loudly as their damaged vocal chords would allow. He didn't approach them or touch them. He simply said, "Go show yourselves to the priests," *and going, they were healed.* Even though they were still leprous as they started out, they didn't allow the pressure of fear to keep them from their "flight" into hope as they walked away from Jesus without immediate tangible evidence of healing (Luke 17:11–14).

God the Holy Spirit lives in each believer, and God has us, no matter what economics, governments, circumstances, or people around us are doing. Jesus said,

> "I've told you these things in advance so that in Me you may have perfect confidence. In this world you have tribulation, trials, distress and frustration [drag and opposition]; but be cheerful, confident and undaunted, for I [the Power] have overcome [lift] the world for you!"
>
> John 16:33

Write Luke 17:14.

_____
_____
_____

Write Philippians 4:13.

_____
_____
_____

Refusing to use circumstances as the benchmark, how can we know we are operating within the will of God?

_____
_____
_____

Identify three areas of opposition in your life.

_____
_____
_____

Identify how that opposition can be beneficial.

_____
_____
_____

Is Transparency in Marriage Biblical?

Dr. Dixie, my husband has attended some men's conferences. I'm grateful for the changes he has made, except for this: he is insisting that we should tell each other everything we think and feel the moment we think and feel it. He calls it transparency. I call it an invasion of privacy. Where's the balance?

—Needing Privacy

Dear Privacy,

Honesty, *openness*, and *transparency* are sometimes used interchangeably. This is confusing because, while related, these words don't mean the same thing.

- Honesty: having integrity, high moral and ethical principles; to be fair, truthful and dependable
- Openness: undisguised, receptive, and accessible
- Transparency: nothing is hidden, but clearly visible and exposed; unprotected

Honesty and openness in marriage is absolutely essential. Trust is imperative for a lifelong relationship to remain strong, and trust can't grow strong in a secretive atmosphere. Clear communication is a necessary part of knowing what another person is thinking because no human being can accurately read another's mind. However, the expectation that everything we think or feel should be immediately exposed to someone else or that they will clearly understand what we've expressed is unreasonable.

The Bible tells us that we are absolutely transparent to God, our Creator.

> The Word of God is sharper than any two-edged sword, penetrating to the division between the soul and spirit, exposing, sifting and analyzing the thoughts and purposes of the heart … not one creature exists that is concealed from His sight, but *all things* are open, exposed, naked to the eyes of Him with Whom we have to do.
>
> Hebrews 4: 12–13

No one can fully discern or understand another person's thoughts and emotions. Sometimes what someone thinks makes us feel good (i.e., "You are the most important person in my life; I can't live without you"). But if we're informed every time they think those thoughts, we can easily become expectant and dependent on being so important to someone else. On the other hand, if we're made aware each time someone is annoyed with us and is "put off" by our thoughts and choices, it will quickly produce a sense of rejection and failure.

Constant unobstructed access into someone else's thought life could be compared to living in a house without inside walls. Because it is completely open, the bathroom fixtures, the back of the refrigerator, and the bed are in full view of anyone from any part of the house. The ugly unfinished backs and sides of the furniture are visible, and there is no place for the inhabitants to have moments of privacy.

"Privacy walls" create a balanced openness, permitting an honest expression of thoughts and feelings combined with a thoughtful refusal to articulate irritated, rude, or impatient thoughts simply because they're there.

Jesus was honest with His disciples and told them everything His Father told Him to share: "I have never spoken on My own authority ... my Father told me what to say and tell ... " (John 12:49). But Jesus was not transparent.

> In Jerusalem ... many believed in His Name, because they observed the signs He was doing. But Jesus, on His part, was not entrusting Himself to them, because He possessed an experiential knowledge of each individual.
>
> John 2:24 (Wuest Expanded New Testament)

Sin has damaged our capacity for "clear as glass" transparency in this world with people. That will change in eternity. For now,

> We are looking in a mirror that gives only a dim, blurred reflection of reality as in a riddle or enigma. But when perfection comes, we shall see reality face-to-face! Now I know imperfectly; but then I shall understand fully and clearly, even as I have been fully and clearly understood by God.
>
> 1 Corinthians 13:12 (AMP)

In your own words, define the differences between *honesty,* *openness,* and *transparency.*

_____
_____
_____
_____
_____

How can *transparency* damage relationships?

_____
_____
_____

How can *honesty* and *openness* build strength into relationship?

_____
_____
_____

From John 2:24, what was Jesus's motive for "withholding Himself" from people?

_____
_____
_____

Write Psalm 19:14.

Why Get Married?

Dr. Dixie, marriage is so outdated. Women have many more financial options now, and men don't seem to have any trouble finding a "sex mate." Why endure the confinement of marriage?

—Don't Need Marriage

Dear Don't,

Americans get married hoping for the following:

- Love
- Sex
- Happiness
- Financial security
- Friendship
- Intimacy
- Children
- Old-age companionship

The problem with making these desires of primary importance in marriage is that when our expectations aren't fulfilled *the way we want them to be*, we abandon the relationship, wistfully looking for someone else who might meet them more fully. The general dissatisfaction in marriage is reflected in reasons why Americans divorce:

- Infidelity
- Physical, emotional, or sexual abuse

- Poor communication
- Change in priorities
- Sexual problems
- Financial problems
- Addictions
- Unmet expectations

God's design for marriage certainly includes joy, companionship, and pleasure. But these enjoyable aspects can only be acquired through the hard work of the following:

- Learning and practicing commitment (Hebrews 10:35–38). This produces emotional and financial stability.
- Learning to love another person more than yourself. Loving as Jesus loves strips away the childish and selfish attitudes of "I want what I want, the way I want it—give it to me *now*." Over time, this yields a harvest of unselfishness and joy (Ephesians 5:25–29).
- Offering respect to someone who is completely different from ourselves and with whom we can't perfectly agree (1 Peter 3:1–5). This encourages acceptance of others.
- Raising children to love God (Malachi 2:15). This produces the old-age comfort of diligent, caring children who mature into diligent, caring adults.
- Becoming more like Jesus each day (1 Corinthians 15:49). This makes our inner righteousness visible in behavior and enhances relationships.

The shelves of books detailing how to find romance and maintain the "positive illusions" described on their pages are longer than how long most relationships last! Many of these books are simply a newer version of *Cinderella*. They may neglect to mention that the necessary process of marriage can be grinding and painful—rather like a rock tumbler that pulverizes the rough colorless exterior so that the beautiful interior becomes visible. Marriage is, and always has been, hard work. It isn't a static one-time event that can be immediately measured, but instead is constructed of the series of triumphs and setbacks called *life*.

The value or necessity of marriage can't be accurately measured by comparing it to singleness, which is often unrealistically depicted as easy, fun, and free from responsibility or discomfort. Rather, a sensible assessment is made by realistically comparing the advantages and disadvantages of being Biblically married or Biblically single and celibate.

Because the combined personalities and beliefs of each couple are absolutely unique, in many ways, each marriage is uncharted territory. Since there is no exact course to follow, couples must keep exploring, sacrificing, and moving forward. An important determining factor between success and failure is whether we view the process of marriage as a burdensome obligation or an adventure.

This doesn't mean that one has to be married to grow up emotionally and spiritually, but because of the lifelong *everydayness* of marriage, those in solid, stable, contented marriages often exhibit more mature levels of unselfishness, willingness to change, share and accept others.

When the inevitable "marriage doldrums" occur, each couple has the opportunity to assess how many of their marriage expectations are fueled by Hollywood. "Marriage melancholy" is a time to ditch the Cinderella illusions. Perhaps couples could watch a good movie together, in which the heroic couple doesn't constantly experience happily-ever-after, but stays together anyway. Couples who stay together discover a strong sense of satisfaction, accomplishment, success, and yes, even happiness!

Write Hebrews 10:35–36.

_____
_____
_____

Write Malachi 2:14–15.

_____
_____
_____

Identify three ways marriage produces maturity and unselfishness.

_____
_____
_____

Identify three ways you are personally willing to change in order to strengthen your marriage or, if single, to prepare for marriage.

_____
_____
_____

Enablement Produces Disablement

Dr. Dixie, the words *enabling* and *codependency* get tossed around a lot. What do they mean? Why is it harmful to be helpful?

—I'm a Helper

Dear Helper,

Helping those in need is a good trait that makes God visible to others. But trying to "guarantee" that the one we're helping never feels unhappy is evidence of a good desire that's out of balance. God often works within the misery of consequences to bring about essential change. We obstruct emotional and spiritual maturity when we constantly minimize the painful consequences of sin for ourselves and for others.

Used negatively, an "enabler" is one who makes it possible—even easier—for another person to continue self-indulgent, destructive behavior. For example, a person might enable a gambler or compulsive spender by lending them money to "get out of debt." Enablers generally believe they are acting out of love to help or protect a person, but shielding the one indulging in destructive behavior from the painful consequences of their choices simply worsens a persistent sin problem.

"Enabling" is part of a larger problem known in psychology as codependence, descriptive of someone who remains in a situation of substance abuse or severe emotional manipulation because *they need the behaviors of the other person.* Codependency describes one who "needs to be needed," "needs" to be a rescuer, "needs" the other person to continue destructive choices so there will be ongoing opportunities to come to their aid.

For example, one spouse is an alcoholic, the other is not. Fighting escalates when the nondrinking spouse announces that alcohol will not be allowed in the house. When the alcoholic repeatedly violates the ultimatum, eventually the nondrinker decides that the fighting is worse than the drinking and resentfully gives in, sometimes even purchasing the alcohol.

God says, "The one who relies on frail people and turns his heart and mind away from the Lord will be cursed with great evil, living like a shrub in a parched, uninhabited salt land." This condition describes the emotional state of both the one with the original problem and the one who encourages the problem to continue. God goes on to say, "But most blessed is the one who trusts, hopes in and relies on the Lord. He shall be like a tree, planted by the river, whose roots spread out and go deep. This one shall not be anxious when drought comes and will not cease to be fruitful" (Jeremiah 17:5–8).

The long-term answer for selfish, out-of-control behavior in any form, *including enablement,* is to lean on the Lord for determination, strength, and wisdom, making choices to stop avoiding or soothing painful consequences caused by destructive behavior.

Wrong enablement produces emotional and spiritual disablement. However, not all forms of enabling are negative. We enable children to grow spiritually and emotionally when we love them and model the love of Jesus. Children and adults are enabled to view themselves as God does when we spend time listening to them with respect and acceptance, reminding them that God says they are important and valuable because they are created in His image. We enable others to reach their highest and fullest potential when we encourage and instruct from the Word of God. This is enabling in the best sense of the word.

> Brethren, take care lest there be found in you a wicked, unbelieving heart, turning you away from the living God. *Instead, admonish, urge and encourage one another* as long as it is called "today" so that none of you may be hardened into rebellion by the fraudulent, delusive glamour of sin.
>
> Hebrews 3:12–13

Write Proverbs 19:19.

_____
_____
_____

Write 2 Thessalonians 3:10–12.

_____
_____
_____
_____

Ask the Lord to show you where you have enabled someone to stay dependent and immature (adult, child, spouse, friend, etc.).

_____
_____
_____

List some ways that you have enabled someone else to reach their God-given potential.

_____
_____
_____

Music Matters

Dr. Dixie, lately I've been paying more attention to country music lyrics. So much of it involves drinking, divorce, and depression. Many seem to think it has no effect on us. Do you think listening to those words affects how we think and act?

—Concerned About Lyrics

Dear Concerned,

A recent study conducted by Rand Corp, a Pittsburgh-based research organization, determined that more than a "catchy" tune seeps into our minds as we listen to music. In a national survey, 1,461 teens were interviewed about music preferences and sexual behavior. Follow-up interviews were conducted one year later and again three years later. They found that adolescents who listened repeatedly to sexually explicit lyrics are almost twice as likely to become sexually active within two years compared to those who do not.

The results were published in the national journal *Pediatrics*. Steve Martina, author of the study, observes, "When kids turn to music media, because the predominant message they get is that women are sex objects, men are relentlessly sexual, and sex is an inconsequential game, they emulate what they hear and are likely to use sex carelessly. The *more often teenagers were exposed to sexual imagery, the more likely they were to engage in sexual behavior* at an earlier age. Based on work showing clear links between lyrics and changing attitudes, *explicit lyrics about sex definitely affect behavior."*

Studies consistently show that the words we listen to, especially when repeatedly reinforced through music and visual images, strongly impact how we think and, consequently, how we act. This principle lies behind the explosion of videos used to promote music sales. Advertisers also obviously know the effectiveness of combining words and music—an annoying commercial jingle may play in the mind for hours after the commercial is over.

The word *music* is almost always used to describe the combining of tonal sounds and words. There is ample evidence that music affects our moods; therefore, it isn't difficult to recognize the link between music and depression, music and joy, music and dissatisfaction with life, wife, or husband.

- Certain types of music have been shown to increase aggression.
- Few would question the romantic impact of love songs.
- Anyone watching a horror movie will appreciate how the soundtrack increases tension and fear.
- Songs from the past can cause memories and emotions to come flooding back.

Information set to music (lyrics) accelerates learning and increases duration of memory. When the information is beneficial—for example, the *Alphabet Song*—music becomes a wonderful teaching tool. However, when the information encourages immoral behavior that is biblically and socially deviant and destructive to relationships, this powerful combination of music and information is terribly harmful.

Words carry enormous power. In Deuteronomy, God declares that repetitively saying and hearing His instructions will determine the quality of life the Israelites and their children will experience.

> Place these words into your soul and heart ... get them deep inside you ... teach them to your children by talking about these words wherever you are—sitting at home; walking down the street; from the time you get up in the morning until you go to bed at night. Inscribe these words on the gates of your cities so that you and your children will live a long time.
>
> Deuteronomy 11:18–21 (MSG)

Shrugging off evidence from both Christian and non-Christian research, insisting that, "I just listen to the music, not the words, so what I listen to doesn't matter" is foolish and spiritually irresponsible. What we listen to repeatedly is recorded into the very center of our being, including the mind and emotions. This determines how we think and feel. How we think and feel determines our choices, and our choices ultimately determine our life experience.

Write and memorize Psalm 19:14.

_____

_____

_____

Write and memorize Proverbs 4:23.

_____

_____

_____

_____

Ask the Lord to show you any part of your entertainment choices that may be affecting you in a negative way.

_____

_____

_____

What will you replace those things with? Be very specific. (Example: I will choose not to watch _____ on TV; instead I will listen to thirty minutes of Christian music.)

_____

_____

_____

Keep a journal of the changes you notice in your thinking and choices.

Anger and Sunsets

Dr. Dixie, preachers say "don't let the sun go down on your anger because it gives the devil an opportunity." My husband is frequently verbally abusive, often just as I'm getting ready for bed. I can't stop feeling angry in a few minutes. Does "giving the devil an opportunity" mean if I die angry during the night, I won't go to heaven?

—Afraid to Sleep

Dear Afraid,

Although there is no distinction made in most English translations, a quick look at the two uses of *anger* in Ephesians 4:26 shows that they are different words. The beginning of the verse indicates that anger is not only permissible, but expected. "When you are angry [*orgizo*], do not sin." *Orgizo* means "an excitement of the mind; a feeling that is justified by the occasion."

The second part of Ephesians 4:26 says "Don't ever let your *wrath* last until the sun goes down." This word is *parorgismos*, a strengthened form of *orge,* meaning "fury, exasperation, or indignation." Vine's Expository Dictionary explains "the sense of provocation [*parorgismos*] must not be preserved or held onto, even though the righteous indignation [*orgizo*] may remain."

Our Father God hates sin in every form, and His holy anger burns eternally against evil that constantly opposes righteousness and justice. When we respond to wrongdoing with that right kind of anger, it reflects

His righteous character. However, if right anger turns into self-defensive resentment, exasperation, and fury because "I" have been offended, sin has entered the picture. We are commanded to let go of that *parorgismos* so that the devil doesn't have opportunity to steal, kill, and destroy (John 10:10).

The mention of *sunset* refers back to Deuteronomy 24:12–15. This part of God's law instructed that all pledges and wages were to be paid by sunset so that no debts were held overnight. Also, throughout the Old Covenant, a great deal of emphasis is placed on what could not be done after sunset at the onset of the Sabbath. While the Christian Church now celebrates the Lord's Day—the first day of the week rather than commemorating the Sabbath on the seventh day—*the principle of rest still applies*. The implication is clear: when we carry rage, bitterness, and resentment day after day and night after night, we will not experience the spiritual, emotional, and physical rest that God promises to His people.

Anger will not keep you "out of heaven" if you have believed in the name of Jesus and have received His gift of life and salvation. Dying with the emotion of anger—even rage and resentment—will not keep you from spending eternity with Him. Our relationship with Him depends on what *He* has done and our acceptance of His life, death, resurrection, and lordship. However, carrying those emotions will affect maturity level and our enjoyment of relationship with God.

You can't make your husband talk differently. He will only be able to choose to change when he recognizes that the verbal abuse is wrong. It may be necessary for you to seek Biblical counsel to understand better how to respond and set good boundaries for your own emotional protection.

But the key to dealing victoriously with such a difficult relationship is understanding how highly God values you as His child. The disrespect and anger from your husband hurts but cannot destroy you as you learn to rest confidently in God's perfect love and power.

> When the goodness and loving-kindness of God our Savior appeared, He saved us, not because of any works of righteousness we had done, but because of His own pity and mercy ... which He poured out richly through Jesus Christ, our Savior.
>
> Titus 3:4–6 (AMP)

Write and memorize Ephesians 4:26.

_____

_____

_____

Write and memorize Proverbs 30:33.

_____

_____

_____

Identify the difference between anger and wrath.

_____

_____

_____

Describe a time when your wrath caused damage in your life.

_____

_____

_____

Describe a time when righteous anger motivated you to right a wrong.

_____

_____

_____

The "Grizzly Bear" of Margin-less Living

Dr. Dixie, I wake up every morning gasping for breath before my day has even begun. I don't know how to do everything that seems required of me. Our two children are deeply involved in entirely different things and I "taxi" them, but we don't get to talk much. My husband and I both work forty-plus hours. I often feel like the guy with a grizzly bear on his back—he doesn't dare stop running, but is too exhausted to keep on. How can I slow things down?

—Exhausted

Dear Exhausted,

You're recognizing that you're living an unsustainable lifestyle, often identified by statements such as the following:

- I can't keep doing this.
- This is killing me.
- It's just too much.

These statements are like flashing red lights; ignoring them spells disaster. If people around you are increasingly commenting:

- You're always late.
- You never talk to me anymore.

- I hardly see you at all.
- You're always so grouchy.

You're probably living a "no margin" life.

A major problem of margin-less living is that all relationships are nurtured in quiet "time margins" where we're focused on people—not activities, work, or video entertainment. When life becomes frantically busy and noisy, relationships always suffer. Satan is far more aware of this than we are! And because Christians usually don't consider constant activity and entertainment to be a bad thing, if Satan can't succeed in making us *sinfully bad*, he will lead us bit by bit into *destructive busyness*.

It takes courage and determination to stand against the eternally unproductive diversions that press around us. We can't withdraw from the necessity of maintaining life, earning a living, and the constant effort involved in teaching and training children. But if we get caught up in the cultural mandate that we have to be entertained and busy every waking moment, we'll become so distracted with nonessentials that relationships will grow weak from lack of nourishment.

Relationships need quiet, undistracted time to grow strong and healthy. Sports and exercise are important for growing bodies, but if all the time you spend "with" your children is in the bleachers, your relationship with them will be stunted. Having fun is an important part of teaching children to enjoy life, but when entertainment becomes the center of life, the result is dissatisfaction, boredom, and the pursuit of "more."

The way to begin getting rid of the grizzly is to place limits on each family member's school or work activities and reduce time spent using TV and computers for passive entertainment. Be reasonable; it will take time for the new plan to produce results. Expect at least some opposition from teachers, coaches, and other parents. If you reduce extra work hours or cut back on volunteer work and church positions, there may be criticism from those whose definition of value depends not upon what God has done for you but how intensely you are "burning out" for God.

Your children, especially those in middle or high school, will feel pressure from friends, which they'll pass on to you. Keep your new goal of building eternally significant relationships—first and foremost, your relationship with God—firmly in mind.

When your "God time" becomes a nonnegotiable priority, other concerns will fall more easily into place. God is for you, not against you! Spending time with Him, realizing His love for you, will give you confidence and courage to face the grizzly as you stop running and throw it off your back.

Write and memorize Ephesians 5:15–16.

_____

_____

_____

_____

Write and memorize Psalm 46:10.

_____

_____

_____

Identify three areas where you need to minimize or eliminate activities.

_____

_____

_____

Describe specifically how spending time with someone enhances the relationship.

_____

_____

_____

Margin-less Living and Irritation

Dr. Dixie, there are so many worried, annoyed people—at home, at work, and for goodness sakes, even in church! I want to be hopeful even when life is stressful, but sometimes their irritation buries me. I know the economy is bad and the world is a scary place, but why do some people treat others like they're the enemy?

—Determined to be Cheerful

Dear Determined,

Here are some practical reasons for irritation:

- People with electronics in the bedroom sleep two and a half fewer hours nightly than seventy-five years ago. This means 45,625 hours less sleep over fifty years. Result: *chronic fatigue.*
- The average office worker's desk is stacked with thirty-six hours of backlogged work; three hours weekly is spent looking through the stacks for needed documents. Result: *chronic frustration.*
- In an average lifetime, we spend eight months opening junk mail and seven years playing phone tag and waiting for latecomers. Result: *chronic annoyance.*
- Americans average ninety minutes daily watching news coverage of Wall Street's

negative performance, local violent crimes and deadly accidents that happen thousands of miles away. This distressing TV exposure is greatly increased during times of natural disasters. Result: *chronic anxiety*

Margin *is the space between your load and your limit.* We are stressed by too much of the following:

1. Activity
2. Rapid change
3. Information
4. Choice
5. Debt
6. Media exposure
7. Electronic connection with people

Our stretched-to-the limit, chronically hurried lifestyle devours margin and feeds irritation. We give the homeless the shelter they need, the hungry the food they need, the short-of-breath the oxygen they need. But we give the margin-less and stressed out what we *don't* need: more constant activity, futilely hoping for distraction.

Jesus offers quiet stillness, *not another activity*: "Come to Me, all who labor and are heavy-laden and overburdened; *I will cause you to rest.* I will ease, relieve and refresh your ... *mind, will, emotions*" (Matthew 11:28).

Margin is breathing room produced by deliberately minimizing nonessentials. It is a deliberately created reserve—no matter how small—of time, money, and energy so the unexpected won't push us over the edge. Margin-less living is the benchmark of our culture; creating margin is counterculture. Margin-less living is the disease of our decade; margin is the cure. Among other things, margin allows the following:

- *More time with God.* Under constant overload, we only react to the pressure. *Margin enables us to think* and to enjoy intentional time with Jesus so we can share God's love with others. If we have no margin and God says, "I want you to do this," our resentful response is "Sorry, God, I'd like to help, but I already have too much on my plate."
- *Better physical health.* We often begin building margin into our lives *after* the health crisis occurs. Our bodies need downtime to recuperate from everyday life. Even the fastest race cars make pit stops for maintenance. A car can't be repaired while traveling two hundred miles per hour! Yet we expect our bodies and minds to be restored while we race through life with never enough time to catch a deep breath. *Margin is essential to good health.*
- *Stronger relationships.* Time spent with spouse, children, parents, and friends builds strength into relationships. Margin-less living is a huge contributor to the collapse of the American family. *Margin allows time to talk, listen, and enjoy one another.* Margin-less living produces irritability that damages family, work, and spiritual relationships.

We don't have to live in constant "survival mode," irritated, stressed out, and struggling to make it through another day. We can choose *right now* to build a buffer into our lives wherever possible. Slow down, simplify, enjoy the benefits of margin, and see what God accomplishes next!

Write and memorize Matthew 11:28–30.

_____
_____
_____
_____

Define *margin*.

_____
_____

Identify three things in your life that produce irritation.

_____
_____
_____

How would breathing room lower the irritation in these areas? (Be very specific.)

_____
_____
_____

Life Should Be Fun, Fair, and Free

Dr. Dixie, in my office, desks are close together. Complaining about money, government, people, houses, spouses, and children AD infinitum is constant. Most of my coworkers say they're Christians. Why don't they sound like it?

—Sick of Bellyaching

Dear Sick,

You work in a cultural microcosm, and what surrounds believers often has a stronger impact on us than we have on it. Consequently, we join in singing the new national anthem: "It's not fair, it's too hard, it's no fun, it shouldn't cost me anything."

When we focus on circumstances rather than God, Christians consider worry and complaining to be unavoidable. After all, life "should" be fun, fair, and free, and when it isn't, we have "no choice" but to grumble.

Complaining comes from an entitlement attitude, which permeates every corner of American culture. Entitlement is produced by *the lie* that Satan told the first couple in Eden: "God is withholding from you. You *deserve* to have that fruit ... You *deserve* to have the same knowledge God has ... You *deserve* to have no limits."

We hear *the lie* constantly from every major system: business, education, government, and religion. Each system uses advertising media to convince us that *the lie* is true:

- You deserve the best vacation, so "for everything else, there's MasterCard ... no payments for two years."
- You deserve to always have fun and excitement, so "buy this bigger, faster, better _____."
- You deserve to always be comfortable, so "ask your doctor if _____ is right for you."
- You were so mistreated—of course you deserve restitution and special treatment. "Call _____ Law Firm to claim your rights today."

Humankind rebelled against God's righteous sovereignty; consequently, what we actually deserve is hell—eternal separation from God. But God's unremitting love, through the tremendous cost of His Son's life, offered mercy.

> The Lord ... merciful and gracious, slow to anger and abounding in loving kindness ... He does not treat us as our sins deserve, nor pay us back in full for our wrongs.
>
> Psalm 103:8, 10 (NASU)

> Why should we ever complain when we suffer consequences or punishment for our sin? Rather, let's examine our ways, and turn back to the Lord.
>
> Lamentations 3:39–40 (TEV)

Fair isn't possible in a sin-contaminated world. However, we can *increase justice* for the genuinely oppressed. Micah 6:7 says, "What does the Lord require of you but to do justly; love kindness and mercy, and walk humbly with your God."

Fun is an important part of enjoying life, but if our choices are dictated by the "fun factor," we will accomplish little of eternal significance. Successful accomplishment, even in difficult tasks, is far more satisfying than the constant pursuit of fun. "A fool's fun is being bad; a wise man's fun is being wise!" (Proverbs 10:23, MSG).

Free is defined as anything that doesn't seem to cost *you* something. *But everything has to be paid for by someone.* "Free money" for real estate loans, "free medical care," and "free college money" all come at great cost to the taxpayer. The only genuinely free gift we'll ever receive is salvation, but it came to us at the immeasurable cost of Jesus's life.

Complaining and grumbling announces the belief that fairness, fun, and free stuff makes life worthwhile, not God. These steps extinguish bellyaching:

- Recognizing that jobs and relationships can be satisfying even when not constantly fun
- Cultivating the mind-set that work is both challenging and a satisfying part of being human
- Acknowledging pain as an unavoidable part of a sin-broken world without giving into it
- Cultivating a grateful attitude for all our blessings

Write and memorize Philippians 2:14–15.

_____

_____

_____

_____

Write and memorize James 3:16.

_____

_____

_____

What is the underlying belief that drives people to complain and grumble?

_____

_____

_____

What is the antidote?

_____

_____

_____

Information Overload and Intolerance

Dr. Dixie, I heard a news story about a man who jumped thirty-five stories, attempting suicide, but miraculously lived when he hit a car and fell into the backseat. He only had two broken legs. When the car owner expressed concern that her car wouldn't be replaced, reporters criticized her for being uncaring. Am I bad because I sympathize with the car owner? I am increasingly intolerant of people who do dumb things to themselves, oftentimes with disastrous results.

—Intolerant

Dear Intolerant,

We live in a world where "breaking news" announces a house fire in Timbuktu fifteen seconds after it ignites. The angry, intolerant emotions you're experiencing are produced by *information overload*. Your impatience isn't necessarily an indication of being *bad;* it does show you lack *wisdom* in what you choose to listen to daily.

We need to ask, "Do I really need to know about this guy jumping out of a skyscraper and landing in a car? Is it really my concern that the car owner seems more anxious about her car than his life?"

I'm certainly not suggesting that we should ignore people's hurts or become callous toward the genuine needs *that we can ease.* But we absorb far too much "news." Information overload becomes frustration when we're repeatedly alerted to needs *we can't meet.* We have the pre-early, early, regular, midday, early evening, evening, late evening, and post–late evening editions of the news. By the time we've listened to forty-seven repetitions of the early morning "breaking news" murder, it seems like we've been informed of forty-seven murders. According to Wikipedia, bad news coverage outweighs good news 69% to 31%. A steady diet of hopeless negativity always produces *anxiety and frustration. Intolerance* toward people comes from hardening our hearts as we try to avoid frustration.

In those times that we can't avoid the negative or pointless news, our first response should be to pray for those caught in difficult situations, even when it's self-imposed. In prayer, we're more likely to see people through Jesus's eyes. Instead of seeing the guy that jumped out of the window as an idiot, we can recognize his hopeless neediness and pray for restoration. And even though we might understand the car owner's frustration that she will have to deal with insurance and out-of-pocket repairs, through the eyes of Jesus, we are more likely to pray that her life perspective will become less self-centered.

When we understand it isn't our responsibility to fix a crisis in Timbuktu, we can pray for those involved and choose to put the situation aside, confident that God is always at work in the lives of people simply because He loves us!

Often we use so much energy being frustrated about people and things we can't change that we have no strength left to spend on what we really *can* change! In John 21, the risen Lord Jesus is conversing with Peter. After asking him three times, "Do you really love Me?" Jesus tells Peter that he will die a martyr's death (verse 18). Peter immediately looks around at John, asking, "What about him?" In verse 22, Jesus' response was very straightforward: "What concern is that of yours? *You* follow Me!"

> If someone falls into sin ... save your critical comments for yourself. You may need forgiveness before the day is out! Stoop down and reach out to the oppressed. Share their burdens, and so complete Christ's law ... each of you must take responsibility for doing your creative best with your own life.
>
> Galatians 6:1–2, 5 (MSG)

Write and memorize 1 Corinthians 15:33-34.

_____

_____

_____

Write and memorize Proverbs 13:20.

_____

_____

_____

What is the difference between ignoring the problems people have and setting wise boundaries?

_____

_____

_____

How can you exercise compassion without becoming "responsible" for every bad thing you hear?

_____

_____

_____

The Sin of Self-Discipline

Dr. Dixie, I've always thought self-discipline is a good thing. But this week I heard a sermon saying that self-discipline is legalism. Now I'm wondering, is it bad to be self-disciplined?

—Wanting to Do Right

Dear Wanting Right,

In the children's movie *Babe*, a runt pig named Babe is offered as a prize to whoever most accurately guesses his weight. Farmer Hogget wins and takes Babe home to his farm where Babe is adopted by Fly, one of Hogget's sheep-herding dogs. Fly's mate, Rex, is the lead sheepdog who has always cared for Hogget's sheep. Under Fly's tutelage, Babe becomes an expert sheepherder. When he wins favor with Farmer Hogget, Rex becomes jealous and angry. He gets into a vicious fight with Fly because she supports Babe. When Hogget tries to break up the fight, Rex bites his hand, and Hogget has to restrain him with a muzzle. Even with the muzzle on, Rex snarls and rages, his eyes burning with hot anger toward Babe, Fly, and Hogget. The vet finally sedates him to calm him down.

Self-discipline is like a moral or spiritual muzzle. The rules of self-discipline insist that we "don't go there," "don't say that," "don't wear that," don't eat that," or "don't touch that." Self-discipline snarls and says,

"Well, I would if I could, but *they* say I can't. So I'll grit my teeth and obey." Self-discipline is proud of how well self keeps the "don't" rules.

Self-discipline may change behavior to some degree for a little while. But the moment determination and willpower weakens, the muzzle comes off and

- we go back to the same old places,
- the old language flows freely again,
- we get our moral "toes" as close to the "don't" line as possible,
- we eat everything in sight.

When we're dieting, even the parakeet isn't safe if self-discipline is the only thing restraining our appetite!

Just before Jesus went to the cross, He told His disciples that He was going away, but He would send the Holy Spirit to take His place. In Galatians 5:22–23, the fruit produced by the Holy Spirit in each believer's life is *self-control*. This essential characteristic of our new nature in Christ operates from "because of who you are, now *do*."

Self-discipline is *self*-effort rooted in the "don't, don't, don't" of legalism, encouraging a "sin conscious" mind-set. Self-control flows out of the presence of the Holy Spirit, and as the believer enjoys this partnership with God, life becomes a joyful "*yes!*" rather than a resentful, grudging "no". Self-control produces a "righteousness consciousness."

> Your old life is dead. Your new life, which is your real life—even though invisible to

spectators—is with Christ in God. He is your life ... that means killing off everything connected with that way of death: sexual promiscuity, impurity, lust, doing whatever you feel like whenever you feel like it, and grabbing whatever attracts your fancy. That's a life shaped by things and feelings instead of by God ... it wasn't long ago that you were doing all that stuff and not knowing any better ... but you know better now, so make sure it's all gone for good: bad temper, irritability, meanness, profanity, dirty talk. Don't lie to one another. You're done with that old life. It's like a filthy set of ill-fitting clothes you've stripped off and put in the fire. Now you're dressed in a new wardrobe. Every item of your new way of life is custom-made by the Creator, with His label on it. All the old fashions are now obsolete.

Colossians 3:3–11 (MSG)

Write and memorize Galatians 5:22–23.

_____
_____
_____
_____

Write and memorize 2 Peter 1:5– 8.

_____
_____
_____
_____

In your own words, define the difference between self-discipline and self-control.

_____
_____
_____

List three results of self-discipline.

_____
_____
_____

List three results of self-control.

_____
_____

Eternal GPS:
God's Positioning System

Dr. Dixie, I don't believe Jesus is the only way to God. Many sincerely spiritual people, confident that they'll have a positive experience after death, don't believe Jesus is exclusive either. A loving God wouldn't make it that hard to get to Him. I believe when we try to do right, the good hopefully outweighs the bad.

—Trusting Good Behavior

Dear Trusting,

Our assessment of how things "should be" comes from a limited human perspective. We've all heard the prideful announcement "If I was God, I'd do this, or I wouldn't do that." But until we humbly recognize we cannot ever know all that God knows, we won't make the *choice of faith* to believe that *God is love, He is always good, He knows all things, and He never makes a mistake.* God's level of goodness is never determined by our level of understanding.

At 6:00 a.m., people look at their respective clocks and agree "it's six o'clock in the morning." We concur with our clocks because there's a specific starting point (Greenwich, England) where time and place are defined for the entire world. All time is measured relative to *Greenwich mean time* (GMT), and all places have latitude (distance north or south of the equator) and longitude (distance east or west of the *Greenwich meridian*) relative to Greenwich. Whether flying, sailing, driving, or walking using a global positioning system, position and time are always measured from Greenwich. If each person decided to use a different starting point for time and place, any meeting would depend solely on chance, with no possibility of success.

We find a constant theme in Scripture: "For God so dearly loved ... that He gave up His only Begotten Son, Jesus. That whoever believes in *Him*, shall not perish, but has everlasting life." This is the profoundly necessary starting point for everything about human existence and how we relate to God. If we ignore this "eternal mean time," our understanding of everything else about life will be inaccurate, based solely on wishful thinking and happenstance.

God doesn't "make it hard." Jesus said we must have uncomplicated, humble faith to receive God's simple plan to enter into relationship with Him (Matthew 18:2–4).

We know without a common unchanging starting point for time and place, chaos would reign supreme in an unguided world. In the spiritual realm, a common unchangeable starting point is even more necessary, and Jesus made it very clear *He is* the "spiritual Greenwich." *He* is that one point from which all eternal existence, security, and order emanate.

> I, Jesus, alone, in contradistinction to all others, am *the* Road, the Truth and *the* Life. *No one comes to the Father except through Me.*
>
> John 14:6 (Wuest Expanded New Testament)

> Jesus is the only One who can save. His name is the only power in the world given to save people. *We must be saved through Him.*
>
> Acts 4:12 (NCV)

> God wants everyone to be saved and know this whole truth: there is only one God, and *Christ Jesus is the only One who can bring us to God.* Jesus became truly human, giving Himself to rescue all of us.
>
> 1 Timothy 2:4–5 (CEV)

Disbelieving Greenwich mean time does not change the reality of its existence. Ignoring it results in violent disorder. Disbelieving Jesus and insisting that "there are many ways to God" will not change the reality that His salvation is the unique gift to humanity that cannot be duplicated or imitated. We can ignore *the truth*, but we do so to our own hurt. And chaos reigns in an unguided world.

Write and memorize John 14:6.

_____
_____
_____

Write and memorize Acts 4:12.

_____
_____
_____

In your own words, explain why Greenwich Mean Time is necessary.

_____
_____
_____

In your own words, explain why a common, unchangeable eternal starting point is necessary.

_____
_____
_____

What do you personally believe concerning relative truth and absolute truth?

Wanna Borrow a Jack?

Dr. Dixie, I usually imagine the very worst outcome. Even when things turn out better than I expected, I'm already so upset by the imaginary "what ifs" that I make a big deal out of everything and can't even enjoy the good. How do I stop doing that?

—Vain Imaginations

Dear Imaginations,

Here's a story that illustrates your dilemma: driving on a country road late one rainy night with his family, Charlie was nearly home when a tire blew out. Opening the trunk, he found the jack missing. He told his wife, "I'll just walk to the neighbor's house and borrow a jack."

As Charlie walked in the cold rain toward the house, he saw lighted windows and thought, *Good. Ned is awake. I'll knock and say, "I've had a flat. Could I please borrow a jack?" And he'll say, "Why, sure! Help yourself, just bring it back tomorrow."*

Suddenly, the light went out, and Charlie muttered, "Oh no! Ned's gone to bed, and he'll be annoyed because I'm bothering him. He'll probably expect payment for his jack. And I'll say, 'Well, it isn't very neighborly of you, but I'll give you ten bucks.' And he'll say, 'You think you can get me out of bed in the middle of the night for ten lousy dollars? Twenty bucks or get yourself another jack.'"

By the time he reached Ned's house, Charlie had worked himself into a rage. Walking though the front gate, he sputtered, "Not a cent more than ten bucks! I have a flat tire, and all I need is a jack. But you're the kind of guy that probably won't let me have one at any price!"

At this point in his imaginary conversation, Charlie arrived at the door and pounded angrily. Ned's head appeared in the upstairs window, and he called down, "Who's there? What do you need?" Charlie yelled, "You and your stupid jack! I didn't want to borrow it anyway!'"

How often we make circumstances worse by our negative imaginings! We create obstacles in our minds and go through life spoiling for a fight, lashing out in a jealous rage at exaggerated offenses, adding imaginary adversaries to the real ones.

Our minds are incredibly powerful. Our thoughts become our choices and life experience. If we observe difficult circumstances and imagine hopelessly that we're going to die buried in the mess, we talk ourselves into that outcome. Hopeless thinking produces hopeless living. Angry, bitter thoughts create an angry, bitter lifestyle that destroys relationships (Proverbs 23:7).

God desires to love us generously, but our thoughts and words often hinder what we can receive from Him. God desired to give the Promised Land to His chosen people. However, focused on their desert surroundings, Israel decided that God couldn't possibly fulfill His promise to lead them into Canaan. Dissatisfied with God's provision, they continually whined and complained about their food, water, and leaders. God reminded them of the power in their words when He said, " As I live, *what you have said in My hearing, I will do*—your dead bodies shall fall in this wilderness ... I will bring your little ones in and they will know the land which *you have despised and rejected*" (Numbers 14:26–32, AMP).

Whatever the situation, when we change our focus to God's tender mercy and His desire to provide for us, our minds will be opened to creative ideas. God's power and His way of thinking will enable us live in triumph over the situation, even while walking through it (Philippians 4:13).

Write and memorize Philippians 4:13.

Write and memorize Philippians 4:4–8.

Identify a time you "borrowed a jack."

How did your thinking make the situation worse?

How will you think/act differently next time? (Be very specific.)

Judge Not! Or Not?

Dr. Dixie, what do you think about people who criticize someone who does things differently than they would? Doesn't the Bible say we're not to judge? Where do they get off telling me I'm wrong? I don't see anyone else—especially preachers—living a perfect life!

—Not Judging!

Dear Not Judging,

This question frequently surfaces in both Christian and non-Christian discussions. "Judge not that you be not judged" is only a partial quote from Matthew 7. The entire instruction given in the chapter is that *before we criticize the splinter of wrong behavior or attitudes in someone else's life, we are to recognize and remove the log of wrong behavior and attitudes in our own life. Only then do we become qualified to help someone else with the splinter.*

Matthew 7:1 is generally understood to mean we should accept others and not be self-righteous since nobody's perfect; therefore, no one is qualified to notice or name sin in anyone else's life. This misunderstanding of Scripture produces toleration of sinful behavior, a problem that is especially grievous within the Body of Christ.

It's true that ministers of the Gospel don't live perfectly, and the Bible clearly states that preachers and teachers are held to a higher standard of conduct with a greater level of accountability when there is failure (James 3:1). However, Matthew 7:1–5 is *not* saying that we must be behaviorally perfect before recognizing sin in others; rather, it is confronting the sin of habitually criticizing others without making a distinction between personal preferences and what the Bible defines as true sin.

> Don't constantly jump on people's failures unless you want the same treatment. A critical spirit will boomerang. It's easy to see a smudge on your neighbor's face while being oblivious to your own ugly sneer. Do you have the nerve to say to someone, 'Let me wash your face' when yours is distorted by contempt? Wipe that ugly sneer off your own face ... to be fit to offer a washcloth to your neighbor.
>
> Matthew 7:1–4 (MSG)

Spiritual ignorance and immaturity steals our confidence in the complete cleansing we received at salvation. The nagging guilt so common among believers makes us feel unworthy to confront sin. "After all," we say, "nobody's perfect. Live and let live." This attitude, coupled with fear of failure and prideful super sensitivity to criticism, creates an atmosphere that makes it very difficult to give or receive spiritual correction and discipline.

Believers are not to criticize the behavior of unbelievers. *We cannot hold an unbeliever to a standard of behavior they've not yet agreed to!* But as the Body of Christ (Romans 12, 14; 1 Corinthians 12), we are to hold each other accountable to the righteous way of life in Christ that *we agreed to* at salvation.

When a big toe is unexpectedly smashed, the body doesn't get mad at the toe. Rather, the body protects the toe and does what is necessary to encourage healing because when that big toe hurts, the entire body feels the pain. When a mature believer calls our attention to sinful attitudes or behavior, it isn't to demean or insult but to protect and encourage healing and growth within the body. This is God's "family plan" for training in righteousness.

Father God desires that we grow up into good spiritual health. As we grow in the confidence of our salvation and in accurate knowledge of what God's Word identifies as right or wrong, our assessment of sin will be based on accurate Biblical truth rather than personal preference.

Write and memorize Matthew 7:1–4.

_____
_____
_____
_____

What has been your understanding of "judge not"?

_____
_____
_____
_____

How does your understanding differ from Matthew 7:1–4? (Be very specific.)

_____
_____
_____

Describe a time that you compromised because you thought it would be judging to disagree or take a stand for what the Bible said.

_____
_____
_____

How can you judge sin without being judgmental?

_____

_____

_____

The Birth of Rage

Dr. Dixie, isn't anger increasing? I dread work because it's always tense. Whenever something malfunctions or the phone interrupts, my coworker curses. My boss seldom smiles. Even in the grocery store, people look anxious and unhappy. People hitting their kids, husbands and wives abandoning their families, road rage, drive-by shootings ...

—Afraid of Rage

Dear Afraid,

Rage isn't new; in the early days of our country, the shootings were ride-by from horseback instead of drive-by from cars. But the level of rage is escalating.

Anger and rage are connected, but different. *Anger isn't sin.* It's a God-given response to wrong, motivating us to make things right. Anger becomes evident *physically* as the body is energized to fight the problem or escape impending danger. But when circumstances stir anger, we must each personally choose between righteous or sinful responses in our thoughts and actions (Ephesians 4:26).

Jesus was a very angry man (Mark 3:5 and Matthew 23). He didn't "get mad"—a selfish anger response—*but He was never without a controlled, very deep anger toward sin and evil, made evident in His compassion for people.* His anger was perfectly righteous and never originated from a prideful defense of Himself or a petulant demand for His own way.

Rage grows out of wrong anger choices when an expectation isn't fulfilled the way we wanted. Children have an immense need for acceptance, harmony, and security. Their primary overriding expectation is that their parents will love them, meeting their physical and emotional needs in a loving home atmosphere. A significant source of the rage in our divorce-torn culture is the terrible neglect of this primary need.

Children are deeply affected by repeated attempts to blend families. Children involved in multiple family transitions quit school, run away, use drugs, become delinquent, and have children of their own before age twenty in much greater numbers than those from stable homes (McLanahan 2005).

A 2009 University of Chicago study found that from 1980 to 2006, the number of married adults decreased significantly. Concurrently, children in single-mother households increased 417%, and children living with neither parent increased 1,440%. In 1998, only 36.4 million American children (51%) lived with two parents. Thirteen million (18%) lived with a single parent, and 22 million (31%) were transient, moving frequently from place to place with other relatives or in constantly changing foster homes. Figures from the recent census will be even more troubling.

The US Statistical Abstract table 76 shows that children living in a single-mother household are twenty times more likely to be fatally abused. As many as thirteen million of the children counted as living with "two parents" have a stepparent, usually stepfathers. These children are seven times more likely to be sexually abused than those living in a family with original mom, original dad, and children that are theirs, not "his" and "hers." Adults who grow up fatherless are twenty times more likely to be imprisoned than adults who grew up with an actively involved father and eight times more likely to commit murder. Rage is filling American prisons.

The number of American children growing up rejected and insecure is increasing. As they enter adulthood, repeated failed attempts to find security from the world around them intensifies their rage. Paul describes the result:

> In the last days ... people will be lovers of self and money, boastful, proud, blasphemers, disobedient to parents, ungrateful, unholy, unloving, irreconcilable, slanderers, without self-control, brutal, without love for what is good, traitors, reckless, conceited, lovers of pleasure rather than lovers of God.
>
> 2 Timothy 3:1–4 (HCSB)

Write and memorize Ephesians 4:26.

_____
_____
_____
_____

What is the "root" of rage?

_____
_____
_____

Read Matthew 23. What is the difference between Jesus's anger and rage as we know it?

_____
_____
_____
_____

"A significant source of the rage in our divorce-torn culture is the terrible neglect of a child's primary need for acceptance, harmony, and security." Do you agree with this statement? Why or why not?

_____
_____
_____
_____

The Solution for Rage

Dr. Dixie, I often hear that Christians shouldn't be angry. But I don't see how I can completely avoid it. Is there a difference between good anger and bad anger?
—Don't Want to be Mad

Dear Don't,

Anger and rage are connected, but different. *Anger isn't sin.* It's a God-given response to wrongdoing, motivating us to make things right. But when our circumstances stir anger, we must each personally choose between righteous or sinful responses in our thoughts and actions. Ephesians 4:26 (AMP): When angry, do not sin; do not ever let your wrath (your exasperation, your fury or indignation) last until the sun goes down.

Rage grows out of wrong anger choices when an expectation isn't fulfilled the way we wanted. It logically follows that if we want to eliminate rage from our lives, we first need to evaluate our expectations. Some are unrealistic and need to be given up. But when we have legitimate expectations that remain unfulfilled, we must *entrust them to God, acknowledging that He is the only One who can fully meet our needs.* When anger arises because of disappointing circumstances, we must choose between trusting God or manipulating people. Our choices determine our quality of life.

Anger energy is often wrongly used to try to manipulate people into the response we want from them. But manipulation consistently fails in the long term, causing anger to spiral into rage. We cannot stop other people from being rude, manipulative, and rejecting, *but we don't have to respond the same way.* That simply escalates the rage. The right response is to let the anger energize us to personal growth and maturity.

Our world defines a powerful person as the one who has the most control over the most things and people. Some words used to describe a powerful person are *big, strong, loud,* or *controlling.*" We are not taught to consider *meekness as power.* Meekness has become equated with *weakness,* but Webster's Dictionary (1848) defines meekness as one who "shows forbearance under provocation." There is no real power in the cowardly manipulation of someone who is smaller or helpless. However, it takes genuine power to say no to the urge to force another into compliance with our own selfish desires.

Matthew 26:50–54 is the account of Jesus's arrest in Gethsemane. The deep hurt and disappointment Jesus felt when Judas betrayed Him and when the rest of His disciples abandoned Him did not culminate in a rage-driven demand that God send seventy-two thousand angels to destroy those who threatened or disappointed Him (Matthew 26:53). Rather, the amazing power generated from a *righteous anger response* enabled Jesus to say no to being rescued from the agony of the cross. Weak? Hardly. His great power, restrained and righteously directed, resulted in the salvation of humanity.

When we, filled with rage because we've been rejected or mistreated, receive the life and love of Jesus through salvation, we are empowered to respond with forgiveness, mercy, and kindness toward others just as Jesus did. But this response doesn't happen automatically. *We have to make choices to restrain rage and temper. This is only possible as we let God fill the need for love and acceptance that people can't meet.*

God is not going to manipulate us like puppets—pull a few strings, and all the disappointment in people will be gone; pull another string, and we'll automatically stop "losing our temper." God gave us a good mind, a powerful will, and His own indwelling Holy Spirit to provide wisdom, power, and authority. Let's stop asking God to do what He said we should *choose* to do for ourselves.

> He who believes in Jesus; trusts in Him and relies on Him shall not be put to shame nor be disappointed in his expectations.
>
> Romans 9:33 (AMP)

Define meekness.

How are anger and expectations connected?

What gives us power to respond with forgiveness, mercy, and kindness?

Write and memorize Romans 9:33 (AMP).

Adrenaline Junkies and Extreme Living

Dr. Dixie, I had nightmares after watching a documentary on BASE jumping and other extreme sports. Why do these people risk being crippled or killed? What's the point?

—Rather Be Safe

Dear Safe,

Generations of Americans have been wrongly taught that we are only highly evolved ape-men, reducing our value to that of "other" animals, with no more hope after death than any ape that dies. Believing that lie, many try to squeeze as much excitement into life as possible, and if the excitement ends in death, "Well, at least we died 'happy.'"

This reasoning contributes to adrenalin-rush choices. If our short futile, difficult life has no particular value, then why not make every minute as exciting as possible? "You only live once—go for the gusto!"

Extreme athlete Karina Hollekim portrays this life view in *20 Seconds of Joy*, a documentary chronicling her dangerous BASE jumping experiences. She searches the world for higher cliffs from which to free-fall, driven by her escalating demand for adrenaline. She said, "I've realized this is my way of running away from the 'mundane' life. Running away is what I'm good at. This is a dream life—not reality. But pretty soon, it's not enough to just jump off a cliff—you have to have more. So I ask myself, 'Does this compulsion finally end when I hit the ground and die?' It's insane. Jumps that we considered safe one hundred jumps ago, we are now making unsafe by flying closer to the ground [in a wing suit] before opening the chute or flying increasingly closer to the cliff wall. Paraplegia is the only thing that could stop me right now."

The average life of a BASE jumper is six years. In 2006, Ms. Hollekim's chute failed to open, and she slammed into the ground at over 100 km/hour, breaking her right femur in four places and splintering her left leg into twenty-one open fractures. She lost over three liters of blood in forty-five minutes.

Amazingly, Karina survived and slowly, painfully regained mobility. In 2010, as she finally returned to the ski slopes, she said, "You have a luck jar and an experience jar. Each time you survive, you take some out of your luck jar and put it in your experience jar. Eventually you run out of luck and hope experience is enough."

Most of us won't jump off cliffs, race motorcycles, or hunt polar bears, but when everyday life loses its edge, our society pushes us to find the excitement we "deserve." We might seek excitement in promiscuous sex or more accomplishments or possessions, perhaps as fanatical sports spectators or through the vicarious excitement of the endless "reality" shows. These always fail in the long term as the excitement grows stale again.

If, however, we focus daily on God's powerful goodness, we will be motivated to eternal accomplishment. The resulting enthusiasm and fulfillment cannot be counterfeited or stolen. Because it depends on God, not people or circumstances, we avoid dependence on the escalating adrenalin demand.

2 Corinthians 4:17–18 and Romans 8:13 (MSG) state,

> These hard times are small potatoes compared to the ... lavish celebration prepared for us. There's far more than meets the eye. The earthly things we see are here today, gone tomorrow. But the things we can't see now will last forever ... if you live according to the flesh, you will die. But if, by the power of the Spirit, you kill the fleshly deeds of the body, you will live.

Life is a precious God-given gift not to be carelessly squandered on superficial and meaningless activities. Shortly before missionary Jim Elliot was murdered by Ecuadorian Indians, he wrote, "He is no fool who gives what he cannot keep, to gain what he cannot lose."

Write and memorize Romans 8:13.

_____
_____
_____

How do you seek an adrenaline rush?

_____
_____
_____

How do you think you can tell when our God-given desire to achieve and excel is spinning into adrenaline rush?

_____
_____

What do you think Jim Elliot meant by his statement "He is no fool who gives what he cannot keep, to gain what he cannot lose"?

_____
_____
_____

Saving, Collecting, or Hoarding?

Dr. Dixie, why keep hand-embroidered pillowcases and nice towels in drawers and never use them? My husband insists that we just use old stuff. Accumulating thrills him. He owns plenty of land but won't sell some so we can be debt-free. Isn't it greed to hoard things? What about Luke 18:22?

—Hate Hoarding

Dear Hoarding,

Hoarding is officially recognized as one of hundreds of anxiety disorders. A new reality TV show explores lives of hoarders whose possessions have become important beyond reason.

The National Institute of Mental Health declares, "Twenty-five million Americans suffer from some form of anxiety disorder, with annual treatment exceeding 60 *billion* dollars." Because these disorders, including hoarding, are increasing, we can reasonably ask, "Are we getting 60 billion dollars' worth of results? Do current treatment programs address the underlying cause?"

Saving for the future is wise; it's a discipline of diligence largely rejected by our instant gratification culture. But if we have money or things allocated for a specific goal—a car, down payment for a house, special occasion, or a mission project—and are unwilling to let go of it when the time comes, *saving has become hoarding.* Hoarding is keeping for ourselves what God has given us to enjoy and share with others, including time, possessions, mercy, forgiveness, and love.

Physical hoarding usually begins with collecting, a hobby that produces genuine enjoyment as items of interest are displayed and shared. Collecting becomes hoarding when acquiring and protecting these things controls every area of life, interrupting normal living. A collector is able to part with a collection; a hoarder is unwilling to use, share, or dispose of whatever is being collected.

Family keepsakes are treasures given to succeeding generations, helping us understand our family history more fully. However, clinging with white knuckles to family memorabilia or possessions—including land— is often evidence of guilt over troubled relationships. When a family member dies, compulsively holding on to their belongings may well be an attempt to alleviate guilt, insisting it shows "how much we really loved each other."

Surrounding ourselves with things we refuse to use indicates a need for security, *but because only God can provide true peace, safety, and stability, "one" of anything will never be enough, and "a thousand" will never be too many* for the fearful, insecure person. This includes money, keepsakes, food stashes, and miscellaneous things that "we may need someday."

The Bible never condemns having possessions, but insists that possessions must never possess us. Matthew 6:24 states, *"No one can be slave of two masters, since he* will ... be devoted to one and despise the other. You cannot be slaves of both God and deceitful riches ... or whatever is trusted in." Luke 12:15 also says, "Watch out! Guard against all kinds of greed; a man's life does not consist in the abundance of his possessions."

The young ruler in Luke 18:18–25 was "owned" by his wealth. Jesus knew that turning loose of his possessions was the only way for him to be free. However, Jesus didn't tell every wealthy person to give everything away.

Hoarding indicates the spiritual problem of unbelief:

- Not believing God will provide for each day's needs (Matthew 6:25–33)
- Not believing Jesus's blood has paid for every relationship failure—past, present, and future (Hebrews 10:10–14)
- Not believing when God says "Give, and it will be given to you ... pressed down ... running over ... (Luke 6:38)

You can't force your husband to change. Pray for him, communicate your thoughts without nagging, and choose to enjoy him. Trust God for determination to love him as he is while God makes the necessary changes in both of you.

Write and memorize Luke 6:38.

_____

_____

_____

Define the difference between saving and hoarding.

_____

_____

_____

Define the difference between collecting and hoarding.

_____

_____

_____

What is God's solution to hoarding? (Read 2 Corinthians 9:6–11.)

_____

_____

_____

Thankful Giving Eliminates Hoarding

Dr. Dixie, why is it so difficult for some people to give things away? I don't understand the unwillingness to spend, share of dispose of possessions. It seems to be a major cause of family destruction when it comes to dividing property.

—Dismayed by Hoarding

Dear Dismayed,

Hoarding is driven by the fear that if we don't hold on to what we have, there won't be enough for tomorrow. It's the decision to stockpile what God has given us to share. Hoarders are controlled by anxiety, and their human relationships slowly suffocate under the unreasonable accumulation and maintenance of possessions.

Givers are distinctively different from *hoarders*. A gift is a voluntary transfer of property requiring nothing in return. Practiced regularly, giving becomes a lifestyle that produces joy in the giver, in the one who receives the gift, and in those who observe the act of cheerful giving. "You'll not likely go wrong if you keep remembering that our Master said, 'You're far happier giving than getting'" (Acts 20:35 MSG).

The good feeling that comes from giving is biological as well as spiritual. The brain actually produces euphoria in the form of dopamine along with oxytocin, a hormone that stimulates love and trust. But real givers don't need neurologists to convince them that generosity is enjoyable, especially when sharing with those in need. Giving promotes good spiritual health.

Active sincere Christianity has always walked hand in hand with generosity. Giving with a gracious heart is a characteristic inherent to the new redeemed human nature, but it has to be cultivated to maturity. Isaiah 58:6–8 says, "God has chosen this fast … to share your bread with the hungry, to bring the poor and homeless into your house, to clothe the naked … and to not ignore [the needs of] your own flesh and blood."

It is certainly not wrong for those who walk with Christ to have and enjoy possessions, but generous, cheerful giving keeps those things in their proper place. Possessions are a necessary part of life but are not necessary for fulfillment and contentment. Paul said, "I'm just as content with little as with much, with much as with little. I've found the recipe for being content whether full or hungry, hands full or empty. Whatever I have, wherever I am, I can make it through anything through the One who pours His power into me."

Jesus deals with the problem of hoarding in Luke 12:15–21: "Be on guard against all greed because one's life is not centered in the abundance of his possessions." Then He told a parable:

> A rich man's land was very productive. He thought to himself, "What should I do, since I don't have anywhere to store my crops? I will do this," he said. "I'll tear down my barns and

build bigger ones and store all my grain and my goods there. Then I'll say to myself, "You have many goods stored up for many years. Take it easy; eat, drink, and enjoy yourself." But God said to him, "You fool! This very night your life is demanded of you. And the things you have prepared—whose will they be?" That's how it is with the one who stores up treasure for himself and is not rich toward God.

Luke 12:16–21 (HCSB)

Holding possessions loosely and growing in generosity is a prominent characteristic in those who love Jesus deeply, while clinging to possessions and money with white knuckles is a predominate characteristic of anxiety and unbelief.

So don't worry, saying, "What will we eat?" or "What will we drink?" or "What will we wear?" For the idolaters eagerly seek all these things, and your heavenly Father knows that you need them. But seek first the kingdom of God and His righteousness, and all these things will be provided for you. Therefore don't worry about tomorrow, because tomorrow will worry about itself. Each day has enough trouble of its own.

Matthew 6:31–33 (HCSB)

Thanksgiving includes *thankful giving* as well as being grateful for what we have.

Write and memorize Matthew 6:31–33.

What is a gift?

Define generosity.

What is God's solution to worry? (Read Matthew 6:24–34.)

Fall Back, Spring Forward

Dr. Dixie, you talk often about growing up spiritually and emotionally. I try hard to make progress in those areas, but it feels like I take two steps back for every one forward. How can I make consistent progress?

—Don't Like Going Backward

Dear Backward,

Because of daylight saving time, we are familiar with the phrase "fall back, spring forward." This phrase describes the experience many people seem to have in the process of growing up spiritually and emotionally.

We have the mistaken idea that if authentic growth is really happening, we won't struggle with any of the "old stuff" anymore, and emotional discomfort will disappear. But if we compare growing up spiritually and emotionally with the physical growing process, we'll quickly see that the discomfort-free perspective is unrealistic.

Let's consider a one-year-old baby learning to walk. The struggle to support himself on legs that wobble and collapse, the pain of repeatedly sitting down hard, the exertion required to learn balance—if the child could fully communicate the discomfort involved in this part of growing up, he would express tremendous discomfort and fear.

While he is mastering the process of walking, he also has to learn to feed himself. Getting that strange appliance into his mouth right side up is difficult enough, but then he has to move the food off the spoon and onto a tongue that simply will not cooperate. Most of the food ends up on his chin and bib. Surely the humiliation and frustration level is great if he could tell us about it!

And then there is the problem of learning to talk. Anyone who has learned a second language understands the struggle of wrapping an uncooperative tongue around sounds that don't make sense most of the time. Then sometimes a word is used that you learn later didn't mean what you thought and understand belatedly why people laughed so hard at a statement that was not intended to be funny.

Growing up consists of assorted triumphs all gained through struggle and discomfort. Staying immature is filled with stagnation, boredom, and defeat. The fact that it's hard and you feel awkward doesn't mean that you're going backward. In fact, it's usually a good indication that you're moving forward into unfamiliar territory, which, after a time, becomes your new comfort zone. Don't become too settled there! God will soon urge you into the new unfamiliar ground that is essential for continued growth.

> Do you see what this means—all these pioneers who blazed the way, all these veterans cheering us on? It means ... get on with it. Strip down, start running—and never quit! No extra spiritual fat, no parasitic sins. Keep your eyes

on Jesus, who both began and finished this race we're in. Study how He did it. *Because He never lost sight of where He was headed*—that exhilarating finish with God—*He could put up with anything along the way: cross, shame, whatever.* Now He's there, in the place of honor, right alongside God. When you find yourselves flagging in your faith, go over that story again.

Hebrews 12:1–3 (MSG)

Jesus never goes backward. "The one who joins himself to the Lord is one-spirit with Him" (1 Corinthians 6:17). Since we are joined with Jesus by His Holy Spirit, we can't go backward either!

It's necessary to acknowledge mistakes and failure, learn from them, and keep growing. But it's important not to dwell on the hardships and discomforts—even the seeming failures. Focusing there only produces the emotional trap of discouragement and defeat. Let's continue to look ahead toward the goal, just as Jesus did.

Write and memorize Hebrews 12:1–3.

_____

_____

_____

_____

Write and memorize Romans 8:28–29.

_____

_____

_____

_____

Identify an area that you *seem to be* going backward.

_____

_____

_____

Recognizing that God is at work even in the difficult times, what do you think God wants to accomplish in you in this stressful or uncomfortable time?

_____

_____

_____

Choosing Peace Instead of Misery

Dr. Dixie, I'm a nervous wreck. I have headaches constantly from tight neck muscles, and I eat antacids all day to keep my stomach settled. It's impossible to have the peace you talk about. There's always something awful happening in the world.

—Always Tense

Dear Tense,

When reading the Bible, we minimize the real stress of the times and how the writers, speakers, and their audiences were feeling at that moment. Political turmoil swirled around Jesus and His disciples as Rome ruled with an iron fist, the emperors demanding to be worshipped. The apostles worked to expand God's Kingdom in a hostile culture that largely rejected Jesus's death and resurrection. The threat of losing lives and property was always present, adding stress to the struggle to earn a living, strengthen marriages, train and educate children, and establish and nourish churches. Sound familiar? What we call the New Testament were letters written to people living in troubled times. The practical counsel found there applies to us as we also live in troubled times.

God promises that when we focus on His unchangeable goodness instead of on the instability around us, anxiety will decrease. That doesn't mean that we pretend there's nothing wrong.

- It means that we won't take all our decision-making information from a world system torn by sin.
- It means that we won't assess our future through the hopeless terror that pours out of the media when disaster strikes and systems fail.
- It means that as we cultivate increasing confidence in God's eternal faithfulness, the inevitable changes taking place around us won't control and destroy us.

> Abraham ... was confidently looking forward to the City which has firm and stable foundations, whose Architect and Builder is God ... while acknowledging and confessing that they were strangers and temporary residents upon the earth.
>
> Hebrews 11:10, 13 (AMP)

In what "city" do you own most of your mental and emotional "property"? God never intended for us to purchase real estate in the Land of Desperation, City of Difficulty, on Depression Street, in the cul-de-sac of Despair. Living there, we sigh and invite "*my* pain, *my* fear, *my* failure, *my* trouble" to move in next door.

In Christ, our Heavenly Father has given His children an inheritance in the Land of Promise, City of Our God, on Providence Road, in the cul-de-sac of Peace and Comfort.

A photographer fills a frame by focusing the camera lens on a specific object. Just so, our minds are filled with our chosen focus. As we develop the habit of trusting God's true unchangeable Word, our "frame" is filled with hope in the midst of despair and joy in an angry world. We live in intentional peace where turmoil is rampant.

Jesus, knowing the fearful circumstances that surrounded His followers as He went to be crucified, said,

> Peace I leave with you; My own peace I now bequeath to you. But not as the world gives ... *do not let* your hearts be troubled ... or afraid. *Stop allowing yourselves* to be agitated and disturbed; *do not permit yourselves* to be fearful, intimidated, cowardly and unsettled. I have told you these things, so that *in Me* you may have perfect peace and confidence. In the world you will have tribulation, distress and frustration; but ... take courage; be confident, certain, undaunted! I have conquered the world and deprived it of power to harm you!"
>
> John 14:27, 16:33 (AMP)

Just before he was beheaded, Paul said,

> Don't fret or have any anxiety about anything, but in every circumstance ... by definite requests, with thanksgiving, continue to make your wants known to God. And God's peace, which transcends human understanding, shall ... mount guard over your hearts and minds in Christ Jesus.
>
> Philippians 4:6–7 (AMP)

Read Philippians 4. How did Paul choose not to have anxiety?

_____
_____
_____

Write and memorize John 14:27.

_____
_____
_____

In which "city" do you own the most property: City of Difficulty or City of Our God? If Difficulty, how do you plan to change locations? (Be very specific.)

_____
_____
_____
_____

If City of Our God, how do you plan to increase your "real estate"? (Be very specific.)

_____
_____
_____

Why Pain?

Dr. Dixie, what's the point of the endless physical and emotional pain of my life? God must enjoy my suffering, otherwise, wouldn't He take it away? I ask Him to, but He doesn't seem to hear me.

—Defeated by Pain

Dear Defeated,

In *The Gift of Pain,* Dr. Paul Brand tells about a young woman born with the condition called *congenital indifference to pain.* Otherwise healthy, she couldn't feel physical pain. At eighteen months, she bit the end of her finger off. Observing her mother's horrified reaction, she quickly learned that to get her own way, she only had to put her fingers in her mouth and threaten to bite.

By age eleven, both legs had been amputated from injuries incurred because she refused to wear proper shoes. Her elbows were constantly dislocated from intentional twisting as she watched dismayed reactions from those watching. She suffered chronic sepsis from self-inflicted infected lacerations on her tongue. By age sixteen, she had deliberately chewed off all her fingers. Rather than learning from her problem and working with it, she manipulated and controlled others through her pain-free existence.

Seen from this perspective, pain is a gift that keeps us from literally destroying ourselves through lack of awareness, disease, abuse, and selfishness. But as Phillip Yancey drily observes, "pain is the gift nobody wants!" (*Where Is God When It Hurts?*)Because pain *hurts*, we spend more time trying to avoid it than investigating what it's telling us.

We wrongly suppose that God's first perfect creation was completely pain-free. But Genesis 3:16 says that sin *increased* pain in childbirth, not *"brought it into existence."* The human body is created with nerve endings for sensation and pleasure; Adam and Eve certainly had the capacity to feel pain. Pain is *intensified* by sin's consequences: disease, injury, and broken relationships. Pain indicates that something is out of order and needs attention. It promotes self-preservation by motivating us to change or eliminate the spiritual, emotional, or physical pain-producing problems.

But pain is also present when positive change begins. Pain announces the joyful onset of childbirth. Pain signals increasing strength when slack muscles are used in a new way. Pain intermingles with the emotional pleasure of a new relationship.

Our good God doesn't smirk at our pain. Even though a loving dad knows a painful skinned knee may later remind the child not to jump the curb with his bike, he doesn't gloat over the pain of the injury. Knowing that lessons learned from the minor injury may later prevent a fractured skull or broken leg doesn't make Dad snicker over the skinned knee. Resentfully believing that God doesn't care makes our pain wasted misery rather than an eternal opportunity to grow in trust.

God would never permit pain's existence in His universe *if pain were only what it looks like to us*. When believers respond constructively to pain *through God's indwelling presence*, we reveal what pain looks like from Jesus's perspective. He faced unimaginable physical and emotional pain, but because He focused on the goal of the Cross rather than on its pain, He could refuse to be controlled by the dread, despair, and anxiety He felt (Philippians 2:5–11).

Christianity uniquely declares that through Jesus, God fully participated in our humanity, giving Him firsthand experience of the pain of rejection, bereavement, physical injury, and despair (Hebrews 2). Jesus paid for our sins so that in the fullness of His good plan, evil, and suffering can be completely eliminated without eradicating the human race.

C. S. Lewis wrote, "They say of temporal suffering, 'No future bliss can make up for it,' not knowing that heaven, once attained, *will work backwards and turn even that agony into glory.*"

How does the "gift of pain" promote self-preservation?

What does pain indicate?

Describe a time in your life that pain produced a beneficial result.

Write Isaiah 61:1–3.

Jesus and Politics

Dr. Dixie, politics fascinate me. I've been told I shouldn't be involved in that corrupt atmosphere, but I think if Christians aren't involved, it'll get worse. Was Jesus involved in politics? Should we be?

—Politically Minded

Dear Politically,

Political involvement is like any other area in which we get to make choices; there's no hard-and-fast rule. Avoiding any profession simply because of the probability of corruption guarantees that we will never hold a job, build a business, or even volunteer! It's true that greed and corruption are frequently a part of politics. But dishonesty, fraud, and wrongdoing also proliferate in medical, educational, and business systems, as well as within religious frameworks.

Jesus remained politically uninvolved because He didn't come to set up an earthly kingdom. His disciples apparently expected Him to work through the established political and religious systems to bring about the change He desired. When He steadfastly refused, they struggled to understand His different approach and, ultimately, for a time, denied Him and fled from the scene of His arrest (Mark 14:48–52).

Even though Jesus didn't hold public office or support a political agenda, He clearly impacted many who were involved in every system simply by teaching them to carry out their legitimate professions, including politics, with an eternal "Kingdom of God" mind-set.

Each individual has God-designed natural talents and supernatural gifts (Romans 12:4–11). Personal interests are developed in the context of growing up. We are given the privilege of choosing how, when, and where to use the gifts. Throughout human history, God has strategically placed His specially gifted people in every moral legitimate profession.

Jesus's ministry included men and women from every walk of life, and He didn't condemn anyone for normal participation in everyday life. Here are some examples:

- *Military*: Jesus didn't tell the Roman centurion to leave the army (Matthew 8:5–13).
- *Medicine*: Jesus didn't tell Luke to stop being a doctor. Colossians 4:14 is evidence of Paul's close friendship with Luke, the beloved physician, who knew Jesus intimately.
- *Religion*: Jesus didn't tell Nicodemus to resign from the Sanhedrin (John 3:1–8).
- *Business*: Jesus didn't tell Joseph of Arimathea, a wealthy businessman, to stop earning money.
- *Education*: Jesus didn't tell the teachers of the law to stop teaching (Luke 2:43–47).

Jesus did say that we are never to depend primarily upon a profession to accomplish what needs to be done or to get our needs met. He told the rich young ruler to give away everything he owned, knowing that the young businessman was "possessed" by his money (Mark

10: 17–23). He told the woman caught in adultery to stop that behavior because it was sin (John 8: 3–11). He made it clear to the Pharisees that their misuse of power and wealth was wrong (Matthew 23:1–5).

Paul's instruction in Colossians 3:17, 23–24 says, "Whatever you do, do all in the name of the Lord," obviously *cannot* include pole dancing, prostitution, murder, or extortion, just to name a few! But it does remind us that God calls His children to be involved in all aspects of life—to bring an awareness of God's love into every area, including politics. Christ followers are called to be salt (Matthew 5:13), preserving, healing, and creating thirst for the things of God. By our presence, we shine the light of God into the very dark places of our world (Matthew 5:14–16).

> God's will and intention is, that by doing right, your good and honest lives should silence ignorant charges and ill-informed criticisms ... live as free people, but don't use your freedom as a pretext for wickedness. Live at all times as servants of God.
>
> 1 Peter 2:15–16

Write and memorize Colossians 3:17, 23–24.

Read Mark 12:13–17. What was Jesus's attitude toward government?

How can God work through you and your profession to further His Kingdom?

Write and memorize 1 Peter 2:15–16.

Choice: Blessing or Curse?

Dr. Dixie, I believe the ability to make genuine choices is part of our likeness to God, and that "choice" was a gift from God in Eden, not from Gloria Steinem in the 1970s. But I'm exhausted by so many options!

—Tired of Choice

Dear Tired,

We generally assume that the increased options provided by American prosperity, allowing us to choose exactly what we want, always guarantee greater happiness. The surprising reality is that *too many options actually create greater distress.*

Recent research reveals that increased choice and wealth have *decreased* the overall spiritual and emotional well-being of Westernized affluent cultures. The US gross national product doubled from 1974 to 2004, but people describing themselves as "very happy" declined by fourteen million (5%). More Americans than ever are "clinically depressed."

Barry Schwartz, writing for *The Scientific American* in 2004, examined responses from two groups who answered survey questions evaluating their level of satisfaction with their decision making. *Maximizers* were determined to examine every option. They engaged in more comparisons, both before and after their selection. Since no one can realistically investigate every alternative, decision making became more frustrating and disappointing as the options increased.

Too many choices raise expectations and deepen the level of depression when expectations can't be met. Determined maximizers were found to be the least happy with the result of their efforts, expressing little pleasure when finding their decision was good and great dissatisfaction when they found a better deal after their selection.

The second group, *satisficers,* stopped looking around when they chose the item that met the need. Schwartz's research shows they enjoyed the results of their decisions more, spending significantly less time brooding afterward than maximizers.

However, both maximizers and satisficers face *adaptation*—becoming accustomed to new things and relationships. For example, a consumer agonizes over which vehicle to buy, finally choosing an expensive SUV. He drives the new vehicle, trying to put other options out of his mind, but familiarity and depreciation soon tarnish the entire experience. He regrets what he didn't choose and is disappointed by what he did choose.

Our lives are crowded with too many leisure and work alternatives, too many consumer choices, and too much information to sort through. We make today's choices by comparing our current options with what we hoped for in yesterday's choices. *But even when we get what we say we want, we discover that the newer, bigger, faster things and new relationships don't satisfy.* Our deep human needs cannot be satisfied by the superficial.

God established the privilege of choice when He planted the Tree of Knowledge of Good and Evil in Eden. We can only reach the full capacity of our God-given human design by making *significant life choices*. When we depend so heavily on *eternally insignificant* choices about cars, clothes, sports, paper towels, and cell phones to make our lives meaningful, we have no time or energy left for the truly significant spiritual and relationship choices that produce human maturity and stability.

In many ways, *we worship the gift of choice rather than God*, Who gave the gift. But when we receive salvation and mature in understanding God's way of *being*, greed and selfishness diminish. The desperate need for more things and greater variety is systematically reduced as we are fulfilled in our relationship with Jesus.

> If anyone ... doesn't agree with the sound teaching of our Lord Jesus Christ that promotes Godliness, he is conceited, understanding nothing ... filled with envy, quarreling, slanders, evil suspicions, and constant disagreement. But Godliness with contentment is a great gain. We brought nothing into the world, and we can take nothing out. *But if we have food and clothing, we will be content with these.*
>
> 1 Timothy 6:3–8 (HCSB)

What is a maximizer?

_____

_____

What is a satisficer?

_____

_____

Which category fits you best? Why?

_____

_____

_____

Write and memorize 1 Timothy 6:3–8.

_____

_____

_____

"Arithmetic" of Worry

Dr. Dixie, my grandmother and my mother were both worriers. I heard them say often that there are things we are supposed to worry about; that it's impossible not to worry. But doesn't the Bible say worry is sin?

—Reluctant Worrier

Dear Reluctant,

When someone tells me "I worry a lot," I suggest they say instead *"I waste much of my time deliberately tormenting myself with disturbing thoughts."* Sounds foolish, doesn't it?

Definition of worry:

1. To tease; trouble; harass with importunity, care, and anxiety
2. To fatigue; harass by pursuit
3. To tear or mangle with the teeth
4. To vex and persecute brutally

By definition, we can see that there's never a time when worry is helpful or beneficial. We nurture disturbing, worried thoughts either through neglect, letting them run through our minds unchecked and unchallenged, or by holding on to them deliberately, supposing that the "load we carry" will generate sympathy in others. However, people eventually respond to our ongoing fretting with annoyance, not sympathy.

Worry takes over when we add, subtract, multiply and divide.

- Worry increases when we *add* more things to an already full schedule, when we *add* pressure to maintain our image, when we *add* others' expectations to each day's agenda. This *addition* produces angry disappointment toward ourselves, God, other people, and life in general.
- Worry increases when we reduce God's available gift of power by *subtracting* God's timing from our requests, *subtracting* prayer from our day, and *subtracting* acknowledgement of God's presence from our crisis or life experience. The assumption that God isn't interested causes us to doubt His unchangeable goodness and mercy.
- We *multiply* worry by imagining "what if," "but maybe," or "this could happen tomorrow." Worry *multiplies* within "always" and "never" statements and in the melodramatic pronouncements "It scares me to death" or "It has happened a million times." *Multiplication* produces terrifying monsters exaggerated out of all proportion.
- Worry grows in the flawed *division* of our lives into "secular" and "sacred." For example, *dividing* work and relationships ("my business") from church and good deeds (God's business) causes us to forget that God is sovereign, always interested and involved in *everything* His children think, do, and say.

Jesus knew we would have ample opportunity to be worried, anxious, and distressed. He and His disciples lived in perilous times. There has never been a time since sin came into the world that peril has not lurked just around the corner. In times of greater affluence or between wars, we're able to ignore the peril more easily, but it never disappears.

Jesus prepared His disciples for difficulties.

> I've told you these things, so that in Me you may have perfect peace and confidence. In the world you have tribulation, trials, distress and frustration; but ... take courage; be confident, certain, undaunted! For I have overcome the world ... I have conquered it for you.
>
> John 16:33 (AMP)

We must each persistently choose whether to worry and nurture anxiety about life or focus on God's good and unfailing promises. Jesus prayed for us (John 17:20) and is praying for us now (Hebrews 7:25). The Holy Spirit intercedes for us continually (Romans 8:27). At salvation, we are eternally joined to God Himself. This gives courage in life's difficulties, *but only if we are focused on God, not the difficulty.*

> Since you have been raised with Christ to new life ... seek the rich, eternal treasures above ... keep your minds set on the higher things that are above, not on earthly things ... for you have died, and your new, real life is hidden with Christ in God.
>
> Colossians 3:1–3 (AMP)

What things have you *added* to your life that increases worry?

_____
_____
_____

Write and memorize John 14:27.

_____
_____

Write and memorize 1 Peter 5:7.

_____
_____

Name three ways you plan to *subtract* worry from your life. Be very specific.

_____
_____
_____

What's Good About Good Friday?

Dr. Dixie, I'm a new Christian. Why do we call the day Jesus died "good"? I'm so glad that Jesus died for my sin and lives to give me life, but saying Good Friday seems to disregard His suffering.

—Sorry for His Pain

Dear Sorry,

Without the perspective of time, Jesus's disciples might also have exclaimed, "*Good* Friday? There seemed nothing good about that day. It was terrifying—the most hopeless day of our lives."

Jesus's disciples watched in despair as the man they had left everything to follow was arrested, manipulated through a secretive midnight trial, and illegally sentenced to die. In their terror, they abandoned Him through sleep (Matthew 26:40), ran from Him (Mark 14:48–52), cursed at those who suspected they knew Him (Matthew 26:69–74), and betrayed Him by silence when He asked for a witness (John 18:20).

Soldiers taunted, "If you are the Son of God, tell us who struck you!" (Matthew 26:67-68). His accusers railed at Him, "Get Yourself down from the cross, and we'll believe in You" (Matthew 27:41-44).

The disciples stood in the distance as Jesus allowed soldiers to nail Him to the cross. The thought must have occurred, "If He is who He claims to be, wouldn't He refuse this horrible death? We share in His Kingdom. What good is a dead King?"

We cannot comprehend the depth of their helpless rage and sorrow as their friend and leader suffered and died that terrible, awful, really bad day.

Over two thousand years gives us a different perspective of that darkest, yet brightest, of all days in human history. Good Friday precedes Resurrection Sunday: Easter. We call it good because the results of Jesus's suffering, death, and resurrection are *very good*!

> God proves His own love for us, for while we were still sinners Christ died for us ... For Christ suffered for sins once for all; the righteous for the unrighteous, that He might bring you to God, after being put to death in the fleshly realm, but made alive in the spiritual realm.
>
> Romans 5:8, 1 Peter 3:18 (HCSB)

Many Christians commemorate Good Friday with the Lord's Supper, remembering Christ's suffering and death for our sakes with gratitude. Jesus's crucifixion and resurrection are the paramount events of the Christian faith; we are instructed to keep them clearly, daily in mind, not just on Good Friday.

"I am laying down My life so I may take it up again. No one takes it from Me; I lay it down on My own. I have the right to lay it down, and I have the right to take it up again" (John 10:17–18 HCSB).

It is pointless to try to find someone to blame for "killing" Jesus. He freely gave up His life. Those who convicted Him and drove the nails simply helped bring to completion the destiny He came to earth to fulfill.

> While we were God's enemies, we were reconciled to Him through the death of His Son ... now, much more, having been reconciled, we will be saved by His life! ... We also rejoice in God through our Lord Jesus Christ, through whom we have received reconciliation.
>
> Romans 5:10 (HCSB)

By accepting Jesus's perfect sacrificial payment for our sin, our right standing with God is assured, and we receive eternal life. And that is why Good Friday, the day Jesus died, is an incredibly wonderful, *very good day!*

Write and memorize Romans 5:8.

_____

_____

_____

Write and memorize 1 Peter 3:18.

_____

_____

Why do we call Good Friday good?

_____

_____

How do you view the death of Jesus—tragedy or triumph? Why?

_____

_____

_____

"Average" Kate Changes History

Dr. Dixie, why all the fuss about Kate Middleton changing history in spite of her "average" upbringing? Average? Really? She has access to enormous power, fame, and money. The rest of us "average" people can't do anything that will make much of a difference.

—Insignificant and Annoyed

Dear Insignificant,

At her birth, Kate Middleton's parents had no inkling that their first child would become the future queen of England. The Middletons have done for generations what "average" or typical people do: grow up, get married, have jobs, have babies, and do life the best they can with the life tools they've been given. As a teenager, Kate learned piano and studied "average" subjects, not knowing that she would one day rank among the world's most famous women.

When Jeffrey Dahmer was born, his parents didn't know that their new baby would become one of America's most notorious serial killers. They too were living their "average" lives as their predecessors had done.

George Washington Carver was born in Kansas Territory in 1864 or 1865, the son of slaves. His father was killed shortly before Carver was born. As a baby,

Carver was kidnapped by nightriders and held for ransom with his mother and brother, who died before they could be rescued. Moses Carver, a compassionate German farmer, ransomed the surviving infant with a $300 racehorse. He had no idea the baby would make the Carver family name world famous.

Carver refused to be a victim. He worked hard to learn, taking advantage of every educational opportunity no matter how limited or difficult. Overcoming abandonment, cultural hatred, and poverty, his eventual life work resulted in the creation of 325 products from peanuts, more than one hundred from sweet potatoes, and hundreds more from other plants. These life-sustaining foods contributed to rural economic improvement around the world, saving lives and enhancing nutritional health for millions.

Who can take credit for his accomplishments? Those who brought Carver's ancestors to America under cruel conditions? The parents who conceived him in poverty? His kidnapper? The God-fearing farmer who ransomed him and nurtured his agricultural interests? Perhaps a kind teacher? Actually, each one of these and many more who touched Carver's life. God does His work through people, and each one, often unknowingly, contributed in some way to the scientific development that improved nutrition for millions. Average people, living life both righteously and unrighteously, were involved in producing this world-changing knowledge.

At your conception and birth, no matter what the circumstances, the structure of the human race was made different because you exist with your unique

DNA. Now, *you get to choose*, not *if* you make changes in world history, but *whether the changes you make as you live your "average" life are constructive or destructive.* We don't have to be rich and famous or wield great power to affect our world in a positive way. We only need to know the love of God and obediently share His love with others. The impact you have on your spouse, children, coworkers, and many more has eternal significance, either negative or positive. There's no such thing as an insignificant life.

> When they observed the boldness of Peter and John and *realized that they were uneducated and untrained men,* they were amazed and *knew that they had been with Jesus.*
>
> Acts 4:13–14 (HCSB)

Write and memorize Acts 10:34–35.

_____

_____

_____

Write and memorize Luke 14:11–14.

_____

_____

Identify three ways you can affect your "world" in a positive way. (Be very specific.)

_____

_____

_____

Do you agree with the statement "There no such thing as an insignificant life"? Why or why not?

_____

_____

_____

From Commoner to Royalty

Dr. Dixie, if I was British, I would probably better understand why it's such a big deal that Kate Middleton was a "commoner" who became a "royal." But isn't that what happens to us when we receive salvation? I think it's a great illustration!

—Born Royal

Dear Royal,

Yes, it's a wonderful illustration of what happens through salvation. Prince William's wife, Catherine (née Middleton), comes from a middle-class background with no aristocratic or titled connections. She's not the first commoner to marry a future king. Elizabeth Woodville, who married King Edward IV in 1464, and Anne Hyde, married to King James II in 1660, were commoners with no direct connections to nobility. Simply by marrying into the royal family, these women, nonroyals by birth, gained aristocratic titles, wealth, and influential, prestigious positions of power.

In a reverse situation, Edward VIII, on being told that he couldn't marry Wallis Simpson and remain king, abdicated the throne in 1936 to marry Simpson less than one year after his ascension. In Jonathon Dimbleby's biography of Prince Charles, the prince recalls the death of Edward VIII and watching Ms.

Simpson pace around his coffin, muttering repeatedly, "He gave up so much for so little" while pointing to herself.

By his own choice, Edward renounced his royal title and position. While their marriage was strong and lasted until Edward's death nearly thirty-five years later, friends observed that the couple traveled and entertained incessantly, apparently to keep regret at bay. The couple lived in exile, mainly in France and the United States because the British government refused to grant Simpson "royal" status. The duke said the difference in titles would force them to be separated at official ceremonies, a condition that was intolerable to him.

When God created the first man and woman, they were royalty by birth. Father-God, Creator and King of all that exists, gave life to them through creation. Satan, appearing in Eden as the cunning serpent, enticed them to renounce their royal position for what appeared to be greater power. To gain what they believed was lacking, they abdicated their "throne," relinquishing their position as Lord and Lady of the earth. Their disobedience resulted in exile from their perfect garden. An angel with a flaming sword (Genesis 3:23) stood at Eden's entrance, guarding the path to the Tree of Life, for if they had eaten its fruit after disobeying, they would have lived forever in their fallen condition.

But God was not satisfied to leave His disobedient royal children in a state of exile. Immediately following their disobedience, God implemented the plan He had designed before creation through His perfect foreknowledge (1 Peter 1:19–20). The plan began in Eden with the killing of animals, their skins covering the naked vulnerability of the fallen Lord and Lady (Genesis 3:21); it continued through the centuries with repeated animal sacrifices and culminated in the once-for-all-time death of God's only Begotten Son (Hebrews 10:9–10). Through the blood of Jesus, God restores all who will accept His gift, reinstating us to the position of royalty and holiness (1 Peter 2:9).

> Since by the one man's trespass, death reigned through that one man, how much more will those who receive the overflow of grace and the gift of righteousness reign *in life* through the one Man, Jesus Christ.
>
> Romans 5:17 (HCSB)

Write and memorize 1 Peter 2:9–10.

What did Adam and Eve believe they were lacking when they chose to disobey God (Genesis 3:1–7)?

Why did God send the first couple from Eden (Genesis 3:21–23)?

Do you believe you are a part of God's royal priesthood? Why or why not?

How would believing you are a part of God's royal priesthood make a difference in your choices and behavior?

_____
_____
_____

Why God Created People

Grandma Dixie, why did God create people if He knew Adam and Eve were going to sin?

—Kiersten

Dear Kiersten,

Many people wonder why God would create people knowing His Son, Jesus, would have to die to pay for sin. It seems like God could have avoided a lot of trouble if He would've just made people *who always had to obey*.

Sometimes we hear that God created us *to serve Him*. After Jesus saves us, we certainly do want to be considerate, generous, and helpful. Jesus tells us that when we are kind, giving a drink of cool water to someone who is thirsty, it's the same as giving Jesus the water (Matthew 10:42)! But God didn't create us to do good things or just to do His work for Him. That would make us slaves with no choice but to work harder and harder for Him, hoping some day to please Him enough. That makes us want to give up.

We are also sometimes told that the reason God created people is to tell others about Him. And when we get to know Jesus better, we are excited about Him and want to tell others about Him. But He didn't create us just to go around the world talking about Him. That would make us simply motivational speakers.

Here is why God created people: He created us so He could love us, so that we could choose to love Him back and, out of that love relationship, do good to others and tell others about Him. But the loving *always has to come first.*

God doesn't *have* love; *He is love* in its purest form (1 John 4:8). God the Father, God the Son, and God the Holy Spirit love perfectly. God fully understands the wonderful advantage of living wrapped up in perfect love. God knows that His love produces unending life, wisdom, strength, and stability.

Even before time existed, God deeply desired to share His perfect love with someone who could *choose to love Him back.* For that reason, God made people so much like Himself that we can walk with Him, talk with Him, and be closer to Him than with any human family member or friend. That ability to choose to love Him means we can also choose to reject and disobey Him. Adam and Eve made that death-producing choice.

God delights in His creation. Every flower and bird is carefully noticed and cared for (Matthew 6:26–30), but those things can't willingly love Him back the way people can. The Bible tells us that since God loves everything He created—planets, stars, plants, and animals—*how much more He loves people created in His likeness.* God is so interested in each detail of our lives that He even knows at any given time how many hairs are on each person's head! "Aren't five sparrows sold for two pennies? Yet not one of them is forgotten in God's sight. Indeed, the hairs of your head are all counted. Don't be afraid; you are worth more than many sparrows!" (Luke 12:6–7).

Even after God's beloved humankind rejected Him, He "so highly prized and dearly loved the world, that He gave up even His only Begotten Son, so that *whosoever believes in Him should have everlasting, unending life*" (John 3:16 AMP). We love because He loved us first (1 John 4:19 HCSB).

Write and memorize John 3:16.

_____

_____

_____

Write and memorize 1 John 4:19.

_____

_____

Our culture often sees people as "intruders" in nature. What does God say about who has greater honor: people or creation?

_____

_____

_____

What should be our attitude toward God's creation?

_____

_____

_____

"Daddy, My Daddy, Sir"

Dr. Dixie, if God really loves us, why would He command us to be fearful of Him? My dad always controlled me with fear. If God wants me to love Him, He'll have to do better than that. I'm not interested in another terrifying relationship.

—Sick of Fear

Dear Sick,

Many respond negatively to "fear of God" because of the brokenness and abuse that has become "normal" for American families. But let's consider *what fear of God is not*.

- Fear of God is *not* the natural panic experienced when danger threatens.
- Fear of God is *not* anxiety or terror. "God has not given us a spirit of fear" (2 Timothy 1:7). "There is no fear in love; but perfect love casts out fear, because fear involves torment" (1 John 4:18). Knowing God's unchangeable love neutralizes the torment of dread.
- Fear of God does *not* mean being afraid of God. Living confidently in God's acceptance of us, in Christ, delivers us from "God fright."

Awe is the attitude created by the right fear of God. *Awesome* originally described God's majesty and tender love and His true power and holiness. Unfortunately, it has been cheapened and is now widely misused to describe fast cars, popular bars, and current stars.

Genuine fear of God gives rise to reverence—the only logical response to knowing God's perfect love and *rightness*. Reverence produces an unworried submission to God. Highly esteeming God generates wisdom, peace, and regard for people who are created in God's image. Sadly, reverence toward God is largely absent in the arrogant, self-sufficient, self-promotional atmosphere of twenty-first century America. Wisdom is not the same as *cleverness*, which often walks hand in hand with evil. True wisdom is *a fruit of the right fear of God* (Proverbs 9:10).

As we nurture *God esteem* rather than *self-esteem*, insecurity is replaced with stability and confidence. Reverence for God frees us from subjection to anything else, including emotional hurt. Focusing on God's great goodness is the remedy for all ungodly anxiety or terror.

Sir is a respectful term used when speaking to someone in authority. *Father* denotes a formal type of family leadership and authority. Jesus often addressed God in Aramaic as *Abba,* which is well translated as "Daddy, my Daddy." This expresses an informal, tender, unafraid relationship. Using these definitions, "Abba, Father" becomes "Daddy, my Daddy, Sir."

God designed families so that children would be loved by daddies (*abba*), loving them back even in the painful times of authoritative discipline (*sir*), which are for our benefit and maturity.

Unfortunately, only a small percentage of American adults have experienced interaction with a lovingly involved, consistent dad in a well-balanced home environment. The good balance between love and the right fear of God has been deeply damaged by the escalating violence and breakdown in families.

Born into God's family, we become the recipient of all the benefits and blessings of Daddy, my Daddy, the King, Sir. Among these are His grace (receiving the good things we don't deserve) and His mercy (not getting the bad things that we do deserve). As His beloved children, we are subject to the loving authority and discipline of Abba, Father, but never abused.

> If God didn't hesitate ... to embrace our condition and expose Himself to the worst by sending Jesus, is there anything else He wouldn't gladly and freely do for us?
>
> Romans 8:32–33 (MSG)

Write and memorize Romans 8:32–33.

In your own words, describe *reverence* toward Father God.

How does violence and brokenness in the home affect our understanding of what God is like?

Describe the difference between self-esteem and God esteem.

The Broken Gospel

Dr. Dixie, church splits and denominations confuse me. I've heard you say, "Sometimes what's sin in Texas is not sin in New York." Why all the disagreement? Where's the unity Jesus prayed for in John 17?

—Wanting Unity

Dear Unity,

Contradictions and disagreements have plagued the Body of Christ since its inception immediately following Jesus's resurrection. Disunity and the desire to impress people grow from selfishness and insecurity. When our comfort zone is threatened, we misrepresent Jesus, our Head, by becoming defensive, antagonistic, and dishonest. Consider this illustration:

> In spite of his habitual stingy dishonesty, Mark sought a promotion and wanted to impress his boss. Aware that the boss's birthday was approaching, Mark initiated a plan. He consulted a clerk at an expensive glassware shop. "Do you have any damaged china, something very valuable, but broken?"
>
> The puzzled attendant checked. "We have an expensive vase with shipping damage that hasn't been discarded." Mark purchased the broken vase for a fraction of its original value, requesting that the clerk wrap it and send it to

his boss. He was confident that when his boss got the gift in the mail, he would blame the damage on the postal service. Mark could then express regret for the damage, receiving good marks for his effort without much cost.

Several days later, Mark called to see if his boss had received the gift. "Yes, I did," his boss replied. "But I'm still confused about why the post office separately gift wrapped each broken piece?" Mark's job was terminated.

The broken vase represents the *good news* that Jesus died and lives again to free us from sin's power. Jesus purchased our freedom at enormous cost. However, through selfishness, mistrust, and fear of others, the "Gospel vase" has been separated into many pieces. Often, instead of embracing a full, complete faith, denominations offer beautifully wrapped fragments of the *Good News*, leaving God's people with a compartmentalized faith that is confusing and limited in power. Pieces of the *Good News* are used to promote an individual or denominational agenda. Hostility and division results when that agenda is questioned.

Tongues, baptism, the role of women within the Body, what constitutes sexual purity, last days, and divorce are a few of the countless areas of disagreement and brokenness. When our focus is on a particular "flavor" of denominational doctrine rather than on Jesus who joins the entire Body together, the Body becomes polarized and legalistic. Adherence to a localized set of rules replaces a balanced view of the whole Gospel. Personal faith becomes individualistic with sharp shards that cut and separate members of the Body. The entire Body is left with far less than God intends for us to have and accomplish.

> Let no one sit in judgment on you in matters of food, drink, feast days, or Sabbath. These are only the shadow of things to come, and having only a symbolic value. But the reality, the substance, belongs to Christ. Let no one defraud you by acting as an umpire, declaring you unworthy ... insisting on self-abasement and worship of angels ... vainly puffed up by sensuous notions, inflated by his unspiritual thoughts and fleshly conceit. *He is not holding fast to the Head, from Whom the entire body ... grows with a growth that is from God."*
>
> Colossians 2:16–19 (AMP)

Read John 17. What is Jesus's greatest desire for His disciples then and now?

_____

_____

_____

Have you experienced a form of division in your church-going experience? In what area? What caused the division?

_____

_____

_____

_____

How could the division have been avoided? (Be very specific.)

_____

_____

_____

Write and memorize Colossians 3:12–14.

_____

_____

_____

Real Men

Dr. Dixie, this may sound weird coming from a guy, but I want to know what the Bible says about what a real man is.

—Tired of Being Compared to Fantasy

Dear Compared,
Movies and commercials *erroneously* teach us that:

- real men fight frequently and viciously without disfigurement
- real men drive cars and motorcycles at dangerous speeds without injury
- real men drink copious amounts of alcohol but never look drunk and stupid
- real men always have beautiful women hanging around
- real men have sex anytime, anywhere, without precaution or consequence
- real men always have plenty of money

This fictitious representation of manhood is as deadly to boys and men as airbrushed fraudulent magazine covers are to girls and women. Trying to measure up to fantasy produces the bondage of promiscuity, alcoholism, eating disorders, and dishonesty.

Our Viagra-soaked culture often describes a real man as one who physically "satisfies" as many women as opportunity presents. However, this actually describes a self-centered manipulator *who satisfies himself upon* as many women as possible.

A dating site offers this perspective: "What separates the boys from men? Of greatest importance is the *ability to independently and successfully handle life's challenges in eight critical categories*—career advancement, transportation, urban/outdoor survival, home renting/buying, manners/etiquette, finance and negotiation, domestic skills, and health, nutrition, and lifestyle." How sad that there is no mention of intimacy with God and integrity, which the Bible says is the essence of manhood.

> Better is a poor man who walks in his integrity than the fool who is perverse in speech ... A righteous man who walks in his integrity—how blessed are his sons after him!"
>
> Proverbs 19:1, 20:7 (NASU)

Jesus was a real man, contrary to paintings from early centuries that often portrayed Him as a slightly feminine wimp. For the most part, this attempt to depict meekness communicated weakness instead.

The Bible accurately portrays Jesus as a cheerful, hard working construction worker who supported His mother and siblings. His skin was sun darkened, and He was lean and muscular from walking miles every day. He was diligent, kind, and humorous, but defended the weak and helpless against the abuse of the unscrupulous with anger that was strong and righteous. Jesus is the perfect example of true manhood.

- real men love Jesus
- real men are diligent and hard working, taking care of those who depend on them, whether money is tight or plentiful
- real men make the continuous choice of monogamy, rejecting the lie that happiness is only found in "variety"
- real men are husbands who don't walk out when marriage gets tough
- real men are daddies who love their children more than they love themselves, refusing the choices that will hurt their children

Obviously, no man is going to keep this list perfectly. The good news is that God doesn't expect perfect, unfailing behavior. However, He deeply desires that *men and women* grow up and stop living from selfish immaturity.

Because we live in a world that is being increasingly trashed by sin, good, determined, godly men who desire to work diligently and love their families may be temporarily blocked from their goal. There is an inordinate emphasis on sex in American culture. As a result, most couples are sexually active before marriage. This is backward from God's design and creates an atmosphere of mistrust very early in the marriage. No matter how determined a young man may be, the sexual history they both bring into their relationship is so negatively powerful, it often destroys the marriage, and children—his, hers, and theirs—are inevitably involved in the breakup. The seeds of destruction sown in extra-marital sexual activity are often stronger than a man's determination to be a good husband and father.

A real man is one who honors women; not using them for his own selfish pleasure. A real man chooses faithfulness to *one wife, until death, giving his life for her* in the same way Jesus loved the Church, His bride (Ephesians 5:25–33). Jesus gave up everything on the cross so that His bride could become all she was created to be.

When the weedy harvest of our past or the culture bears fruit in the lives of men who really want to do right, the only solution is to go back to the basics:

- receive salvation
- let Jesus be your friend and mentor
- learn about God's design for marriage and parenting

As unpopular as it is to talk about men being dependent on Jesus for making wise decisions and for living a life that is stable and strong, *it really is the only way.*

A frequent argument against this statement is "I know men who go to church all the time, and they're no different than anyone else!" Well, of course! Going to church doesn't change a man into a mature Christian any more than standing in the middle of a garage saying "*varoom, varoom*" will make him into a motorcycle!

Church is a good starting place, but it is the man who spends time alone with God every day, learning to know God, receiving wisdom, strength, and renewed determination to live with integrity, who becomes a real man.

A real man patterns his life after Jesus, allowing the Holy Spirit to lead and empower him. Living out of God's original design is what makes a man *real*.

(These questions apply to both men and women. Women, consider the questions in context of how you think about your spouse and how changing your thinking will change your relationship.)

Which of the erroneous statements about men have you believed? What effect has that had in your relationships?

_____

_____

_____

Define the difference between meekness and weakness.

_____

_____

_____

_____

Choose one of the attributes of Biblical manhood. How will making choices from this attribute change your relationships?

_____

_____

_____

_____

Write and memorize Ephesians 5:25–29.

_____

_____

_____

_____

In your own words, define what you have believed makes a real man.

_____
_____
_____
_____
_____

In your own words, define a real man from God's perspective.

_____
_____
_____
_____

How does premarital or extramarital sex negatively affect a marriage relationship?

_____
_____
_____

Write and memorize Hebrews 13:4.

_____
_____
_____

Real Women

Dr. Dixie, I watch teenaged girls struggle to become women in a culture that isn't very friendly to true femininity. How can I explain to my granddaughter what it really means to be a woman?

—Struggling for Words

Dear Struggling,

In years past, girls and women were considered to be the gentler more "mysterious" gender, generally treated with careful respect, especially when pregnant or accompanied by young children. On the negative side, those same days also forbade women to vote or own property because they were not believed to be intellectually capable.

Women have fought hard over the years to reestablish the equality purposed by God when He created the first man and woman. Many improvements have been made in the areas of salaries, sports, property ownership, and leadership opportunities. But with the gains, we have lost so much feminine gentleness: the awe and joy of being a woman, a wife, and a mother— *in that order, according to God's design.*

Movies, commercials, and magazines *erroneously* teach us that

- real women are always thin and flawlessly beautiful

- real women (just like "real men") can drink copious amounts of alcohol without looking drunk and stupid
- real women always have a man
- real women *want* to have sex anytime, anywhere
- real women have glamorous, powerful jobs and plenty of money

This fictitious representation of womanhood has resulted in the bondage of promiscuity, alcoholism, eating disorders, and revolving door relationships that are systematically destroying American children.

In the early 1960s, a seemingly innocent trend known as the unisex movement began to grow. Clothing, hairstyles, and names became more generic so that male and female distinctions became increasingly blurred.

The word *unisex* literally means "one sex" or "one gender." While male and female human beings have many things in common—for example, eyes, arms, legs, heart, liver, kidneys, etc.—there are many physiological, emotional, and life-perspective differences. These differences *cannot be neutralized through medication or by wearing look-alike clothing and pretending we're the same.*

God created us, *male and female*, and designed that in marriage we become *one flesh*. However, He never intended that we try to become *one gender*. Here are two examples of many *unisex attempts*:

- Boys are expected to sit and learn in classrooms *just like girls*. When they don't—*because they can't*—medication is too freely used.

◄ Women are expected to be straightforward, black-and-white thinkers *just like men*, and when they aren't—*because they can't*—their more overt emotions are labeled and medicated.

1 Peter 3:3–5 (MSG) says, "What matters most isn't your outer appearance ... but your inner disposition. Cultivate inner beauty, the gentle, gracious kind that God delights in."

- ◄ real women love Jesus
- ◄ real women are diligent, nurturing relationships with husband and children
- ◄ real women make the continuous choice of monogamy, rejecting the lie that happiness is only found in "variety"
- ◄ real women are wives who don't walk out when marriage gets tough
- ◄ real women are moms who love their children more than they love themselves, refusing the choices that will hurt their children

A real woman appreciates men with their differences, rather than disdaining them because they aren't like her. A real woman chooses faithfulness to *one husband, until death*, putting her own needs and desires second to the needs of her dependent children (Proverbs 31:10–31).

Obviously, no woman is going to keep this list without failure. God doesn't expect perfect behavior but desires that *men and women* grow into spiritual and emotional maturity. A real woman patterns her life after Jesus, allowing the Holy Spirit to lead and empower her. Living out of God's original design is what makes a woman *real*.

(These questions apply to both women and men. Men, consider the questions in context of how you think about your spouse and how changing your thinking will change your relationship.)

Which of the erroneous statements about women have you believed? What effect has that had in your relationships?

_____

_____

_____

Choose one of the attributes of Biblical womanhood. How will making choices from this attribute change your relationships?

_____

_____

_____

_____

Write and memorize 1 Peter 3:3–5.

_____

_____

_____

_____

Unisex is not a Third Gender

Dr. Dixie, I think that our "sexually free" culture has actually increased confusion about true gender differences. Women often seem aggravated or ashamed about the way God designed us. How can we teach our daughters to be excited about being a woman?

—Promoting Femininity

Dear Femininity,

From creation, God predetermined a gender-specific function of womanhood: the ability to bear and nurture children. Because of the impact of Adam's rebellion, this is a part of God's design that sometimes doesn't operate as He planned. Infertility and spontaneous miscarriages were not a part of God's original blueprint.

However, even with the built-in equipment and the intrinsic desire and ability to nurture children, girls must be *guided to maturity by older women in order to fulfill* that design the way God intended, in much the same way that musical ability has to be trained to become really great (Titus 2:3–4).

When role models are predominately TV single moms, girls don't know they are to look forward to marriage and motherhood—*in that order*—and are unprepared for the challenges they will face. Girls have to be *taught* that godly husbands and children are gifts from God. They have to be *taught* that husbands and children are *family* and that cats, dogs, and parakeets are *pets* and that these categories are not interchangeable.

In our eagerness to reestablish gender *equality*, we have wrongly pursued *sameness*. Women often resent that "men expect women to be just like them," while feeling angry because men aren't like women! Blurred gender lines and unisex thinking increases the confused frustration.

Another *misguided unisex belief* is that men and women are *the same except for anatomy*; therefore, real women will want to have sex as often as men. This misbelief results in a great deal of disappointment and blame as he discovers that her enthusiasm for physical intimacy is *different* than his and believes it's "just her." As long as he believes the lie, he will constantly be looking for another woman who will do for him what he believes "all women except his wife" will do.

One result of unisex thinking is that women try to neutralize the natural consequences of sexual activity—pregnancy. The morning-after pill and abortion are in greater demand than ever. But when a woman embraces abortion as an acceptable solution, even if she never personally chooses it for herself, she develops an unnatural hard-heartedness. Both women and men have suffered terrible loss through this erosion of compassion toward the small and helpless.

Women are generally nurturing and emotionally sensitive. But as gender distinctions become more blurred and young girls are not taught how to be themselves *within God's design*, the percentage of women who abandon, abuse, or kill husbands and children is on the rise, indication of an appalling cultural change.

When the weeds of cultural influence and personal sin bears fruit in the lives of women who really want to do right, the only solution is to go back to the basics:

- ◄ receive salvation
- ◄ let Jesus be your friend and mentor
- ◄ learn about God's design for marriage and parenting from our "owner's manual"—the Bible

As unpopular as it is to talk about women being dependent on Jesus for making wise decisions and for living a life that is stable and strong, *it really is the only way.*

The verse 1 Timothy 3:11 states, "For women [like men] must be worthy of respect and serious, not gossipers, but temperate and self-controlled, thoroughly trustworthy in all things." (AMP)

(These questions apply to both women and men. Men, consider the questions in context of how you think about your spouse and how changing your thinking will change your relationship.)

In your own words, define what you have believed makes a real woman.

_____
_____
_____

In your own words, define a real woman from God's perspective.

_____
_____
_____
_____

How does the misuse of pregnancy negatively affect a woman's emotional well-being?

_____
_____
_____

Define two major differences between men and women (not physical). Why is "unisex" so destructive?

_____
_____
_____

Write and memorize Titus 2:3–5.

_____

_____

_____

Does God Have A Favorite Gender?

Dr. Dixie, I often struggle with the feeling that women are somehow less valuable to God then men. If God loves everyone the same, why would He create us unequal?

—Wondering

Dear Wondering: Through the centuries, women have lived under the burden of misbelief that Eve's sin somehow condemns her daughters to a position of disgrace, silence and lesser value. Even today within the Body of Christ, the inaccurate, but very prevalent belief that Eve was cursed by God permits domination, abuse and the silencing of Godly, gifted women.

A careful reading of the Genesis account shows us that God cursed the serpent. He then told Adam that his disobedience had subjected the soil to the curse of decay and malfunction always linked with sin. God did not curse His beloved humankind. He sorrowfully told them that by their choices, they had placed themselves under the deadly consequences of sin. These consequences included the battle to earn a living by frustrating toil and sweat; an ongoing power struggle between men and women and the painful sorrow of watching children grow up in a sin-contaminated world (Genesis 3:14-19).

Jesus' earthly life showed that every man and woman of every ethnic background, age and economic scale is of equal value. When we kneel at the foot of the Cross, recognition of that equality is to become a part of our daily lives.

> For as you were baptized into Christ ... you have clothed yourselves with Christ. There is now no distinction neither Jew nor Greek, there is neither slave nor free, there is not male and female; for you are all one in Christ Jesus.
>
> Galatians 3:27-28 (AMP)

God does not play favorites. It is the sinful, fleshly desire to dominate that gives birth to prejudice and the devaluation of another person because of gender, skin color, language or age.

In Luke 10:1-3 we read that Jesus appointed 70 "others" of His followers to go into the "harvest field" of lost humanity. He cried out, "The workers are few! Pray the Lord of the harvest to send forth laborers!" It seems ludicrous to suggest that He would only accept male volunteers, either then or now. Jesus never treated women as less gifted, spiritual or accepted than men. When He addressed His mother, or those who followed Him as "woman", it was in the vocative case—directly addressing a person. "Woman" is not a term of reproof or severity, but of endearment and respect.

When Jesus launched His public ministry, Salome, mother of James and John; Joanna, the wife of Herod's household manager; Susanna, Mary Magdalene and other women—along with the men—gave up lives of "normal" home-bound comfort to become Jesus' disciples, traveling with Him, serving Him and giving from their financial means as they learned how to minister, side by side with Him. (Luke 8:1) Mary, sister of Lazarus, "sat at the feet of Jesus" (Luke 10:39). This is a phrase commonly used to describe a *disciple; one who follows and learns from a teacher.* The same phrase is used to describe the response of the man from the region of Gerasenes who was delivered from a "legion" of demons (Luke 8:26-35), and who was sent by Jesus to "go back to your home town and tell all that God has done for you" (Luke 8:39).

On Resurrection morning, Mary Magdalene was the first to arrive at the open tomb and to proclaim to the other disciples that Jesus had risen from the dead. The women who mourned His death had the first joyous privilege of announcing His Resurrection.

Women from the time of Eden, those who saw the open tomb and now 21st century Christian women can live joyfully out of the resurrection message that the ground is level at the foot of the Cross. When we receive eternal life and enter into partnership with God, we are individually able to hear from *Him* how He wants us to minister to others. Criterion is not gender, skin color, language or age. It is simply to love God wholeheartedly and walk in obedience to *Him*.

What was Jesus's attitude toward women? Give examples.

_____

_____

_____

_____

In your own words, describe the requirements to be a "worker in God's field":

_____

_____

_____

Name five women who were acquainted with Jesus, and describe how they contributed to His ministry:

_____

_____

_____

_____

_____

Write and memorize Galatians 3:27-28:

_____

_____

_____

Prejudice Is A Two-Way Street

Dr. Dixie, I belong to a "minority." Last week, I discovered that I'm in the minority even in the "minority" group! In a discussion, I reacted to disrespectful comments made toward people of another culture. When I said, "prejudice goes both ways," I was really surprised by the contempt directed toward me! Please clarify what prejudice is.

—Accepting of Others

Dear Accepting: The dictionary defines prejudice as "an unfavorable opinion formed without knowledge, thought, or reason; unreasonable feelings, hostile opinions, or attitudes regarding a different religious, economic or national group."

Racism is a word often associated with prejudice, but its use indicates a sad lack of understanding about humanity. There is only one earthly race—*human*. Within that one race, there's great diversity in skin, hair and eye color; height, weight, personalities and belief systems. Within that one race, there are two genders: male and female. "Uni" or "trans" is not a third gender. Because there is only one race, an *inter-racial* relationship doesn't exist unless someone has married a space alien! It's an *inter-cultural* relationship.

Yes, prejudice is a "two-way street". Prejudice is the expression of unfavorable opinions formed in ignorance, fear and the narrow-mindedness of selfishness and pride; demonstrated in hatred and contempt toward *any differences in any area*. Prejudice assumes that anyone who disagrees with "us" is, of course, ignorant, jealous and wrong.

Here are a few—of many—common prejudicial statements. How many of these do you believe?

- Women are less capable than men
- Men are less capable than women
- Rich people are greedy
- Poor people are lazy
- Political conservatives are close-minded and non-progressive
- Political liberals are immoral
- Red-heads have bad tempers
- Blondes aren't too bright
- Christians are intolerant hypocrites
- Non-Christians are maliciously evil
- Thin people can eat anything they want
- Obese people have no self-control
- Dark-skinned people are violent
- Light-skinned people are arrogant
- City people are soft
- Country people are uneducated hicks

Each one of these statements describes characteristics that can be found within every group. However, prejudice grows from lumping an entire group of people together, assuming we "know" how *everyone within the group* thinks; why "they" do what "they" do; and that we fully understand how and why "they" feel as "they" feel.

This is a presumptuous attempt to play God. God truly does know all things about all people. We don't. Scripture takes a very dim view of favoritism and prejudice.

> For suppose a man comes into your meeting wearing a gold ring, dressed in fine clothes, and a poor man dressed in dirty clothes also comes in. If you look with favor on the man wearing the fine clothes so that you say, "Sit here in a good place," and yet you say to the poor man, "Stand over there," or, "Sit here on the floor by my footstool," *haven't you discriminated among yourselves and become judges with evil thoughts*
>
> James 2:2-4 (HCSB)

> For as many as were baptized into Christ ... you have clothed yourselves with Christ. *There is now no distinction: neither Jew nor Greek, there is neither slave nor free, there is not male and female; for you are all one in Christ Jesus.*
>
> Galatians 3:27-28 (AMP)

We who know Jesus are to set the example by our acceptance of people in every circumstance and culture, especially the unsaved, while at the same time, not tolerating the sin of prejudice in our own lives.

Why is the word "racism" incorrect when describing the problem of prejudice?

_____
_____
_____
_____

In your own words, define prejudice:

_____
_____
_____

Ask the Lord to show you areas of prejudice in your own life that you may have considered to be "just normal thinking":

_____
_____
_____
_____
_____

Write and memorize James 2:2-4:

_____
_____
_____
_____
_____

Our Declaration of Dependence

Dr. Dixie, I'm glad to be an American citizen, and grateful to enjoy the freedoms we still have. But it seems that so much freedom is being stolen by those who don't understand what real freedom is. Please explain the difference between freedom and "no rules."

—Concerned American

Dear Concerned,

Americans enjoy the Fourth of July with fireworks, time away from work, and a nationwide display of American flags. This fun and excitement is the celebration of freedom.

Freedom means different things to people. To some, it's the privilege of voicing opinions and voting our choice for public office. To a prison inmate, it's the ability to live without constant supervision. To one confined by a debilitating illness, freedom means good health. To those who ignore civil laws and do whatever they want how, when, and where they want to do it, freedom means no rules, limits, or accountability. But this is an illusion; *true freedom never means that there are no limitations*.

Romans 6:16 says, "You are the slaves of him to whom you continually surrender yourselves, whether obedience to sin, which leads to death, or obedience to God which leads to righteousness and right behavior."

Freedom is not a question of *whether* we will be under authority. *Freedom is simply the privilege of choosing whom or what we will obey.* When we commit ourselves to controlling others, acquiring more things, or the wrong use of sex and chemicals, the initial sense of unlimited freedom always ends in terrible bondage. Obeying God may initially seem *restrictive* but is actually *protective*, producing genuine joy and freedom in Christ as we display His "flag" of love, truth, and peace every day.

> You have been set free from sin's bondage and have instead become obedient to God ... resulting in eternal life. Remember, the wages which sin pays is death, but the bountiful free gift of God is eternal life in Jesus Christ our Lord.
>
> Romans 6:22–23

Webster says, "Freedom is the power to act, speak, or think without *externally* imposed restraints." Traditionally, Americans are independent—a character quality essential for building this great nation. However, an independent spirit and self-regulating mind-set results in lawlessness when each person disregards others and begins to "do what is right in his own eyes" (Judges 17:6). The rejection of absolute truth creates spiritual and moral darkness and a disordered, chaotic life experience.

True freedom is found in Godly wisdom that *imposes* internal *restraints on thoughts, actions, and words.* The genuinely wise person considers the significance of words and consequences of behavior before speaking or acting. Final choices are evaluated through the unchangeable truth of God's Word. Jesus is that truth.

Disciples of Jesus Christ have declared their dependence on Him, acknowledging that we are helpless and unable to accomplish anything of eternal value if unconnected to the life of Jesus, the Vine (John 15:5). This admission is difficult at first because we have learned to believe that dependence is shameful and weak. We believe the lie that if we try harder, talk louder, and work smarter, we can fix whatever is wrong in our lives. This illusion is maintained by our small "successes" along the road to ultimate failure.

Acknowledging and declaring our dependence on Jesus makes His power available *internally* so that we are able to walk through life *externally* confident and filled with His wisdom—truly free!

> Jesus said to those who believed in Him, "If you hold fast to My teachings and live in accordance with them, you are truly My disciples ... you will know the Truth, and the Truth will set you free. So if the Son liberates you, then you are really and unquestionably free."
>
> John 8:31–32, 36 (AMP)

According to Webster, what is true freedom?

_____

_____

_____

How do we find true spiritual freedom?

_____

_____

_____

_____

Does it seem contradictory that in order to be free, we must declare our dependence on God? Why or why not?

_____

_____

_____

_____

Write and memorize John 8:31–32, 36.

_____

_____

_____

_____

Do You Sit in the Cellar or Perch on the Porch?

Dr. Dixie, people repeatedly say, "I can't help what I say. That's just how I feel!" Well, maybe we really can't help how we *feel*, but I don't think most angry people would talk to their families the way they do if Billy Graham was in the same room. So how do we keep from losing it since Reverend Graham doesn't live with us?

—Wanting Consistency

Dear Consistency,

I think we would all agree that emotions and tornados have some things in common. Okies react to tornado warnings in several ways: run for the deepest, strongest safe room and stay there until the last raindrop falls; stand in the front yard with a video camera until the wind becomes so violent standing is impossible; or even scream defiantly at the storm, determined not to submit to the brutality of the approaching tornado.

There are similar reactions to the profound emotional hurt and disappointment experienced in the "storm" of betrayal, abandonment, or tragedy. Some bury their hurt or anger in the deepest, strongest "safe room" they can find inside themselves. *We call them stuffers.* These people appear *from the outside, for a time,* to be controlling their emotions.

Others may stand in the "front yard" of their lives, recording and replaying the "video memory" of the hurt, screaming into the storm. In their determination not to give in, they constantly express their hurt, rage, and frustration to anyone who comes near. *We call them dumpers.* These men and women, because of the *obvious lack of control,* are often labeled with some form of emotional disorder.

Even believers fall into these categories, unaware that we who are saved by Jesus have a third option. After all, unlike Reverend Graham, *Jesus does live with us all the time.* So instead of stuffing and becoming a walking "garbage can" or instead of spewing our rubbish out on others, we can give our emotional storms to Jesus. When we unload our garbage into His bottomless Dumpster then listen quietly while He reassures us of His love and His unlimited power to protect and provide for us, emotions that would otherwise swing constantly from low to high will become increasingly stable.

There are some physical conditions that can make controlling emotions more difficult, including thyroid, blood sugar, and hormone imbalances, and it may be necessary to address these medically. But even then, by God's strength in us, we can choose to restrain outbursts of selfish temper and words. Persistent lack of self-control has no place in the life of an adult *who has received salvation in Christ.*

If we live, talk, and act out of how we feel with no restraint, out-of-control emotions will create disaster. Our owner's manual, the Bible, explains the connection between the brain, emotions, and mouth and indicates clearly that because we are created in the likeness of Almighty God, we *can act differently than we feel.*

A self-confident fool utters all his anger, *but a wise man holds it back and stills it* ... when I was a child, I talked, thought, and reasoned like a child; now that I have grown up, I am done with childish ways *and I have put them aside* ... for I can do all things through Christ Who pours His strength into me.

Proverbs 29:11, 1 Corinthians 13:11,
Philippians 4:13 (AMP)

Are you a stuffer or a dumper? How do you respond to hurt? (Be very specific.)

_____
_____
_____
_____

Do you think it's acceptable to "dump" on Jesus? Why or why not?

_____
_____
_____
_____

Do you think the statement "Acting differently than you feel is obedience, not hypocrisy" is true or false? Why?

_____
_____
_____
_____

Write and memorize Proverbs 29:11.

_____
_____
_____

Tornadoes and Emotions—Twins?

Dr. Dixie, emotions are so volatile! Why would God give us something that causes so much trouble?
—Would Rather Not Feel

Dear Rather Not,

Seasoned Okies are watchful when thunder rumbles, knowing that a sunny sky can become black and dangerous in a matter of minutes.

Emotions are a "storm threat" every bit as dangerous as a tornado, but because we really don't understand them, we believe that emotions cannot be predicted or controlled. If we think emotions are our authority, we'll feel obligated to obey them. "I just couldn't help myself," we mutter defensively. Or "He makes me so mad" is a common evaluation after an emotional outburst. The truth is: our authority is God and His Word, not emotions.

Emotions are predictable because emotions always follow thoughts. If we think bitter, enraged, resentful thoughts, within moments, the predictable storm clouds of a bitter, enraged, resentful emotional "tornado" will develop. When we choose kind, forgiving thoughts instead, our emotions will gradually change to fit our new way of thinking. *Emotions can only be controlled by controlling our thoughts.*

Paul repeatedly emphasizes the importance of controlling and changing our thoughts:

> We are destroying speculations and every lofty thing raised up against the knowledge of God; *we are taking every thought captive to the obedience of Christ* ... do not be conformed to this age ... but instead *be transformed by the entire renewal of your mind* ... by its new attitude.
>
> 2 Corinthians 10:5, Romans 12:2 (AMP)

God never tells us to do something that is impossible to do in partnership with Him. So we can be confident that as we know Him more accurately and depend on His power more fully, we *can choose* forgiveness over bitterness even when we don't feel forgiving. We *can choose* kindness instead of resentful, jealous thoughts even when our emotions don't feel kind. This is faith in action.

The acrostic OVER helps us better understand how to get over emotional storms:

1. O–Observe which emotion you are experiencing. Is it hurt? Envy? Rage? Frustration? Christians often define an "unacceptable" emotion (for example, rage) by one that seems more acceptable (hurt). It is important to be honest about our specific emotion. This takes practice *and is for our benefit, not for God's information.*
2. V–Verbalize to God first, not people. If we take our emotional reaction to people first, the

explosion will cause damage. If we give them to God first, releasing our emotions on Him and receiving what we need from Him, we are far less likely to explode on people when the time comes for discussion.
3. E–Evaluate what your emotions tell you about your thinking. *Remember that thoughts produce emotions.* Emotions make invisible thoughts visible to others. As you become aware of your thoughts and listen to what God has to say about the situation, He will enable you to change any thought patterns that are Biblically wrong and harmful.
4. R–Resolve to make decisions according to what you hear from God, not according to how you feel. Find scriptural support for what you're hearing from God, being careful not to use just one verse (proof texting) but find overall principles and instruction from the entire Word of God.

Psalm 19:14 (HCSB) says, "May the words of my mouth and the meditation of my heart be acceptable to You, LORD, my Rock and my Redeemer."

Do you think the statement "Emotions are predictable because is emotions always follow thoughts" is true or false? Why?

_____
_____
_____
_____

Write and memorize 2 Corinthians 10:5.

_____
_____
_____

Write and memorize Romans 12:2.

_____
_____
_____

Practice the OVER acrostic in three situations.

1.
_____
_____
_____
_____

2.

3.

God's Stimulus Package

Dr. Dixie, my husband and I work hard. A *big* birthday party for us is to go to a local restaurant and spend $50—and we have to save to do that. I constantly have a knot in my stomach when I hear the news about the selfish, lavish, personal, and government spending going on at our expense. I don't want to make myself sick. I need to know how to stop being so mad about the "stimulus" madness.

—Enraged

Dear Enraged,

Stimulus is something that *gives incentive and spurs us into action.* It's a word currently used to describe strategies aimed at jump-starting a world economy collapsing under a burden of dishonesty and rampant greed.

This isn't a new problem, although it certainly seems to be escalating. Americans in the postwar Roaring Twenties focused on getting more things and enjoying new inventions and fads. Industry became capable of producing vast quantities of goods. But since economic growth could only continue if consumer demand increased, people had to be persuaded to abandon old-fashioned habits like savings accounts and buying what they needed only when they could pay for it.

"The key to economic prosperity is the organized creation of dissatisfaction," the president of General Motors declared in 1929. Advertising strategies that were originally developed to rally support for World War I shifted toward persuading people to buy automobiles and household appliances. Many who wanted these products didn't have enough money to buy them. This gave rise to another "innovation." *Chronic consumer debt*, euphemistically called "credit", was born. But credit only postpones the inevitable day when debt-laden consumers can no longer purchase unless someone raises their credit line. When school, church, legal, and government offices are filled by those who believe unlimited spending and credit is a personal right guaranteed by the Constitution, a national and global crisis is inevitable.

We can't ignore the crisis and should pay close attention to the decisions of elected officials. But to avoid living in anger and hopelessness, instead of focusing intently on the irresponsible activities that we can't change, we must choose to focus on what God says He is able and willing to do, no matter what the economic conditions are. God's unchanging stimulus package offers a proven alternative: "The key to true prosperity is the organized creation of generosity, contentment, and self-control."

- Our culture insists that prosperity is "getting all we can and 'canning' all we get." God says greed and hoarding is idolatry. Generous giving is the antidote: "He who sows sparingly and

grudgingly will reap sparingly and grudgingly; he who sows generously ... will reap generously and with blessings" (2 Corinthians 9:6, AMP).
- ◄ Our culture claims that a bigger "credit line" indicates prosperity. God says, "Debt produces bondage ... the borrower becomes the lender's slave" (Proverbs 22:7, NASV).
- ◄ Our culture demands instant gratification. God says, "When you pursue My Kingdom first, you'll be given all that you need" (Matthew 6:33).
- ◄ Our culture says, "You owe me." God says, "Give, if you want to receive. And with the measure you use when you confer benefit on others, it will be measured back to you" (Luke 6:38, AMP).
- ◄ Our culture whines, "You have to give me what I want whether I work or not." God says, "If a man is not willing to work, he is not to eat either" (2 Thessalonians 3:10, NASV).

Greed, dishonesty, and entitlement guarantee the enslavement of individuals and nations. God's plan guarantees provision and freedom.

In your own words, describe how you have been affected by this mind-set: "The key to economic prosperity is the organized creation of dissatisfaction."

_____
_____
_____
_____

Which of the above cultural beliefs has had the greatest affect on you? In what way?

_____
_____
_____

Write and memorize Matthew 6:33.

_____
_____
_____

Write and memorize 2 Corinthians 9:6.

_____
_____
_____

Untwisting Twisted Thinking

Dr. Dixie, you talk about how we're supposed to think so often, sometimes I think your "record is stuck"! But it's actually beginning to make sense to me. Can you give me five easy steps to new thinking?

—Wanting Change

Dear Change,

I'm glad the repetition is working! I can't give you *easy* steps because while changing the bad habit of wrong thinking isn't *complicated*, it can be *hard work*. However, here are several harmful thought habits to watch for, along with new thought habits to practice. The more consistently you apply the new "thought regimen," the more quickly you'll enjoy good changes in your life experience.

1. *Black-and-white thinking* is perfectionism that allows no gray areas. It sees everything as absolutes: wonderful or worthless, right or wrong. *Renewed thinking accepts, without resentment, that there are variations and exceptions in every area of earthly life.* This is not relativism. It's simply an acknowledgment that we're all at different levels of maturity and understanding in our unique situations.

2. *Overgeneralization* draws sweeping conclusions about situations and people with little evidence. This results in anxiety and resentment. *The renewed mind carefully considers all available facts, through a grid of God's mercy, before coming to a conclusion.*
3. *A negative mental filter* strains out all positive information and affirming words. *Renewing our minds, accepting ourselves as God accepts us in Christ, allows us to receive both praise and criticism, without being destroyed by either.*
4. *The mind reader* imagines that it's possible to know accurately, at all times, what other people are thinking. This results in defensiveness, rejection, and brokenness. *The renewed mind refuses to "play God," accepting that only God knows the mind of each person* (1 Corinthians 2:11).
5. *Awful-ism* magnifies difficulties while minimizing the good in situations and achievements. This thought habit exaggerates isolated events, emotions, mistakes, and imperfections. *A renewed mind, agreeing with God's Word, maximizes the good, and minimizes the failures* (1 Peter 4:8).
6. *High expectations* expressed in "should, must, shouldn't, ought, and can't" statements indicate rigid internal rules about what "has to" be done. *The thought habits of a renewed mind offers grace and mercy, just as Jesus has given us* (John 13:34, 2 John 5).

7. The *labeler* applies negative tags such as *stupid, idiot, imbecile, loser, jerk,* or *pig* to himself and others. *The renewed mind recognizes that every person has intrinsic value because we are created in the image of God.* Jesus said, "Whatever you do to the least of these, you have done to me." (Matthew 25:40) That "whatever" includes name-calling.
8. The *personal blame mind-set* accepts responsibility for every negative event, even those over which he has little or no control. *A mind in agreement with God refuses to take responsibility or blame for someone else's choices.* (Matthew 23:37)

What we believe at the very core of our being will dictate whether we enjoy or despise the one life God has given us.

- Beliefs form our thoughts and words.
- Thoughts become emotions.
- Emotions, in our culture, largely determine our choices.
- Choices determine habits.
- Habits determine the quality of our life experience.

Our thinking has been distorted and perverted in a world system cradled in the lap of the evil one (1 John 5:19). *It's essential that we know God's Word and consistently pay attention to our thoughts. To be free from distortional thinking, we align our thoughts with God's Word* (Romans 12:1–2, 2 Corinthians 10:4–5).

Identify two of the eight harmful thought habits that most influence your daily life:

_____
_____
_____
_____

How have they affected your life experience? (Be very specific.)

_____
_____
_____
_____

Write and memorize Colossians 1:21–22.

_____
_____
_____
_____

Write and memorize Romans 13:14.

_____
_____
_____

I Can't Stop Thinking "I Can't"

Dr. Dixie, I have many bad habits I want to break, but when I try, I hear myself thinking, "I can't" constantly. Help!

—I Can't Quit

Dear Can't,

Breaking the habit of thinking "I can't" is the essential first step to freedom from any bad habit—for example, foul language, complaining, physical dependence on some*thing*, or emotional dependence on some*one*. Eliminating "I can't" is especially necessary for anyone who claims a relationship with the Lord Jesus based on Philippians 4:13: "I can do all things in Christ Who empowers me."

We've heard about the law of attraction, mind over matter, and you are what you think. Each points to the same thing: *thoughts create our overall life experience.* Although there's always the risk of misapplying this concept, it is firmly based on biblical truth. Proverbs 23:7 states, "For as a man thinks within himself, so he is."

Thoughts that are reinforced through constant repetition become deeply ingrained thought habits. When we tell ourselves over and over "I can't," "I don't know," "I'm confused," or "I'm too tired," we come to believe the statements as inescapable truth. Because decisions flow directly from these thought patterns, the life experience will inevitably reflect increasing failure, ignorance, confusion, and a weary, foot-dragging apathy.

The good news is that these sinful, destructive thought patterns can be changed. Here are four steps to move from the hopelessness of "I can't" into the joy-filled life of "together, God and I can."

1. Ask the Holy Spirit to call your attention to how often you think and say some form of "I can't." Carry a notebook everywhere the first week and write your "I can't" thoughts as soon as you become aware of them. Write the thought exactly as you think it. These will include thoughts like "This won't work," "I don't have time," "It's too hard," "I'm too tired," or "It's too much trouble."
2. Positive affirmations may temporarily reduce "I can't" thoughts, but any "positive thinking" not undergirded by the truth of God's Word will quickly lead to becoming positively discouraged! Replace each "I can't" thought with Biblical truth. For example, "I can't get everything done. There's not enough time" would be replaced with "Lord, thank You that I'm invigorated and strengthened ... according to Your mighty power, so that I am able to exercise endurance, patience and perseverance, with joy" (Colossians 1:11).

3. When we learn to believe "I can't," *everything seems impossible*, and we stop trying. In 2 Corinthians 3:4–6 (AMP), it says, "This is the confidence we have through Christ ... our power and ability and sufficiency are from God. He has qualified us, making us to be fit and worthy and sufficient." Just think! Since God Himself has made us sufficient, *the only thing lacking is our decision* to "do it anyway" and "do it afraid" until we experience success.
4. As you begin *by faith in God's power* to do what you once believed to be impossible, keep a record of your successes. Noticing even the small successes encourages you to keep growing and changing. The more you practice, the more you'll see that you can do what you previously thought you couldn't.

There's really no such thing as "I can't" for anyone who has received the life of Christ. Our refusal to try is a clear statement of "I won't," usually because we're afraid of failure, discomfort, and inconvenience. Fear paralyzes. Understanding God's perfect love neutralizes our immature selfish fear of risk so that we can march out with confidence to accomplish what God desires to accomplish in His partnership with us.

Identify two harmful thought habits you discovered (as you carried your notebook) that most influence your daily life.

_____
_____
_____
_____

How have they affected your life experience? (Be very specific.)

_____
_____
_____
_____

What Biblical thought habits will you replace them with? (Be very specific.)

_____
_____
_____
_____

Write and memorize Philippians 4:13.

_____
_____
_____

The Lord Gives ... and the Lord Takes Away?

Dr. Dixie, we've experienced a tragic death in our family. We've heard various versions of "The Lord gives and takes away. His ways are beyond our understanding." I know people intend to comfort us, but that statement enrages me! Is God really responsible? Who can we trust if God takes our loved ones away from us?

—Grieving

Dear Grieving,

This statement is often used simply because people feel helpless in tragedy and don't know what to say. Comfort is the intent, but because it implies "God kills people," it prompts despair instead.

Job was a wealthy man from Uz, a righteous, powerful man of integrity. Job experienced horrific tragedy: in one day his livestock was stolen, his servants were killed, and all ten adult children, perhaps with their families, died when a storm destroyed the house where they had gathered.

> Then Job ... tore his robe and shaved his head. He fell to the ground and worshiped, saying: "Naked I came from my mother's womb, and naked I will leave ... The Lord gives; the Lord

takes away. Praise the name of the Lord." In all this, Job did not sin or blame God for anything.

Job 1:20–22 (HCSB)

Remember that there's a difference between what the Bible *reports* and what it *endorses as Truth*. Job chose to praise God, no matter what, but it appears that he believed God was *the cause* of loss *since God didn't stop it* from happening. That's a common misunderstanding in our time as well: "God can do anything. *He could stop it if He wanted to.*"

- Is God the cause?
- Does God really give, then take?
- Do we study the life of Jesus, who said, "Anyone who has seen Me, has seen the Father … I and the Father are one" (John 14:9, John 10:30)?
- Or do we study Job's words, who had only heard of God but didn't actually know Him, and said, "Surely I spoke of things I did not understand" (Job 42:3, 5)?

Jesus is the place to look for an accurate understanding of God's character, *not Job*, because Jesus "is the sole expression of God's glory … He is the perfect … image of God's nature, maintaining, and guiding … the universe by His mighty word of power" (Hebrews 1:3, AMP). Jesus came to reveal God, the extraordinary Giver, who never takes back His gifts (Romans 11:29).

> God is not a man, that He should tell or act a lie … that He should feel repentance for what

> He has promised. Has He said and shall He not do it? Every good and perfect gift is ... coming down from the Father of the heavenly lights, who does not change like shifting shadows.
>
> Numbers 23:19, James 1:17 (AMP)

The sin of Adam brought sickness, tragedy, and death into God's perfectly designed universe. God is bringing to completion His plan to eradicate all sin and its effects. Meanwhile, God promises that *He will always bring benefit out of any and every situation* for those who love Him (Romans 8 28).

Jesus came to

- be our friend (John 15:15)
- take away the sin of the world (John 1:29)
- destroy the works of the devil (1 John 3:8)
- carry our worry and anxiety (1 Peter 5:7)

He is the exact reflection of God, who is the Father of compassion and the God of all comfort (2 Corinthians 1:3).

This doesn't sound like someone who would kill, steal, and destroy. Rather, Satan is our bitter enemy, who is a murderer and father of all lies (John 8:44).

How do you understand Job's statement "The Lord gives and the Lord takes away"?

_____
_____
_____
_____

When have you said or heard that statement? What affect did it have on you?

_____
_____
_____
_____

How do you think your life experience would change if you were no longer afraid that God will "take away" from you?

_____
_____
_____
_____

Write and memorize 1 John 3:8.

_____
_____
_____

Does God Take or Receive Our Loved Ones?

Dr. Dixie, there have been four deaths in my family in a very short time—one expected, the other three tragic and unexpected. Why so many in one family? Why won't God let me heal up before He takes someone else?

—Bereaved

Dear Bereaved,

We often hear the statement in times of death that God has "taken" someone home to be with Him. We say, "God took my husband" or "God took my child to heaven." Some try to justify God "taking" a young person by explaining that "God needed a bright smile in heaven" or "God needed another angel in the heavenly choir." A particularly cruel statement is a line from a poem, often found on the back of funeral flyers: " ... God broke our hearts to prove He only takes the best."

But if we really listen to those statements, it makes God sound unbearably selfish. God, who creates and owns all things, needs a bright smile more than a mother needs her daughter? Or more than a husband needs his wife? Hardly. And truly, even if God "needed" another singing angel, He would have to create one because no human being will ever become an angel. We are gloriously human for all eternity.

God doesn't "take" people. *Death, the destructive result of sin in the world, takes people from this earthly life.* 1 Corinthians 15:26, says, "The *last enemy* that will be abolished is death." Because of God's unremitting love for humankind, when His children succumb to that last enemy, He tenderly *receives* us into His presence to be endlessly loved and fulfilled.

God experienced the agony of watching His beloved Son die. He is able to comfort, at the deepest level, those left with gaping holes in the fabric of their lives. This is one reason it's so important not to lay the responsibility for unexpected or tragic death at God's feet. If we believe He caused it or refused for some unknown reason to stop it when He "could have," our resentment will prevent us from receiving His tender comfort and strength.

Why so many in one family? That's a question no one can accurately answer because our human view of life is so limited, and we drain important energy trying to reason it out. It's far more worthwhile to use that energy to deepen our faith in the goodness of God.

Grieving becomes more complicated when facing the incredibly painful loss of more than one family member. For a time, life may feel hollow and hopeless; you may feel a longing to join your loved ones. Perhaps you don't know which person to grieve for first or most; you may feel guilty because you miss one more than another. With losses so great, it's hard to believe that something so terrible could happen and leave you still alive, lonely and disoriented without the familiar family structure.

Realizing that grieving multiple losses may take longer, lean deeply into God's tender limitless empathy; join with other grieving family members and close friends for strength and comfort. Allow time to mourn the loss of each person separately. Be generous with yourself, realizing that merely enduring is enough for a while until the hope and joy of a "new normal" gradually returns.

> Blessed be the God and Father of our Lord Jesus Christ, the Father of mercies and God of all comfort, *who comforts us in all our affliction so that we are able to comfort any afflicted with the comfort with which we ourselves are comforted by God.*
>
> 2 Corinthians 1:3–5 (NASU)

Describe a time that you experienced the loss of a loved one and wondered why God "took them" away from you.

_____
_____
_____
_____

Did it make you doubt God's goodness and love? Describe your thinking during that time.

_____
_____
_____
_____

Why is God able to understand the pain of grief and loss we feel when someone we love dies?

_____
_____

Write and memorize 1 Corinthians 15:21–26.

_____
_____
_____
_____
_____

The End Is Near!

Dr. Dixie, I've always heard that no one, not even Jesus, knows when the end of the world will be. If Jesus doesn't even know, how do people think *they* can predict the day and hour?

—Annoyed by Presumption

Dear Annoyed,

Over the centuries, countless attempts have been made to pinpoint the time of Jesus's return described in Matthew 24:32–33, 1 Thessalonians 4:15, and other scriptures as well. Many *recorded* failed predictions of Christ's return range from AD 30 to the present. Their failure is obvious because we're still here. In 2011, Harold Camping predicted that the Rapture would occur at 6:00 p.m., May 21, 2011, and that the world would be totally destroyed by October 21, 2011. The predominate prediction in 2012 is based on the abrupt ending of the Mayan calendar; giving rise to predictions that the world will end December 21, 2012.

The exact time of Jesus's return is unknown and unknowable to people, although the Bible gives information about the general social and economic conditions that will precede His coming. Scripture assures us that Judgment Day will occur with Christ's return (John 5:28–29, Revelation 20:11–15). Yet the Bible clearly says that the exact time is unknown and cannot be predicted. Mark 13:31–32 tells us that even though heaven and earth will pass away, God's unchangeable Word will stand forever. Then comes the statement that creates some confusion: "But of the day and hour, no one knows—not the angels in heaven, nor the Son, but the Father Himself."

It's important to remember that during Jesus's thirty-three years on earth, He lived life fully human, like us in every way, deliberately choosing not to respond to life at any time from His God nature (Hebrews 2:17, Philippians 2:6–7). Understanding this, Jesus's statement really is no more difficult than in Luke 2:52, where we learn than Jesus "increased in wisdom and stature." This indicates that as a human being, having chosen not to draw upon His all-knowing, all-powerful, everywhere-present God nature, *His knowledge was finite during His time on earth.* As a human being, He didn't have knowledge of future events unless given to Him specifically by the Holy Spirit. Now that Jesus is seated on His heavenly throne, operating fully in His omniscience, of course He knows the date of His return! We don't.

We should invest our time in preparing ourselves and others for Christ's return, not trying to calculate the exact moment it will happen. Pope Innocent (1284), Dr. H. L. Wilmington (1524), William Miller (1884), Hal Lindsey (1970), and countless others have attempted to pinpoint the day and hour. Many predictions have been highly publicized, and some have rationalized their error by saying, "If it helps people get ready, then this is worthwhile, even if it didn't happen."

Unfortunately, this disobedience causes weak believers to doubt and gives the unsaved another opportunity to mock the Bible as unreliable and God's children as hopelessly gullible.

Jesus calls us to faithful obedience and spiritual sobriety. We are to be spiritually alert, not idle, presumptuous, or apathetic.

> Concerning that day or hour no one knows—neither the angels in heaven nor the Son—except the Father. Watch! Be alert! For you don't know when the time is coming ... It is like a man on a journey, who left his house ... gave each one his work, and commanded the doorkeeper to be alert. Therefore be alert, since you don't know when the master ... is coming ... Otherwise, he might come suddenly and find you sleeping. And what I say to you, I say to everyone: Be alert!
>
> Mark 13:33–37

What have you learned to believe about the end of the world, both when and how it will happen?

_____
_____
_____

Why do you think people try so hard to guess when the end will come?

_____
_____
_____

Read Mark 13:33–37. What is the emphasis in this passage?

_____
_____

Read Luke 19:12-26. What has Jesus, the "nobleman," given you to invest during this time of waiting for His return? How have you invested?

_____
_____
_____

Mayans and the End of Time

Dr. Dixie, there's so much talk about the Mayan calendar ending on December 21, 2012. After Harold Camping's fiasco, I ignore most of it. But this calendar thing has a ring of truth to it. Are we close to the end?

—Not Sure

Dear Not Sure,

Doomsday talk about December 21, 2012, has become huge on the Internet, cable TV, and religious programming, spreading nervous fanciful speculation like wildfire. Many unrelated groups have joined the anxious chorus, including Nostradamus advocates and a wide variety of eschatological Christians, Native Americans, and spiritualist sects, all discussing the Mayan calendar and wishfully predicting that 2012 will usher in a new age of happiness and spiritual growth. As with every wave of fear, there are many Christian and non-Christian opportunists achieving financial security by selling survival manuals and dried food for a future that supposedly doesn't exist! Do we see a contradiction here?

Numerous doomsday scenarios are presented by those fearing bombardment by large comets or asteroids, some expect a reversal of the earth's magnetic field, and others expect severe solar storms associated with the eleven-year solar cycle, which may peak in 2012. A major theme is celestial alignments as the sun will supposedly line up with a galactic center on December 21, 2012, subjecting us to mysterious deadly forces.

If we connect the conjecture with *only the first part* of a scripture like Luke 21:25–26, it's easy to see why people become anxious. Jesus said, "Then there will be signs in the sun, moon, and stars ... there will be anguish ... among nations bewildered by the roaring sea ... People will faint from fear and expectation of the things that are coming on the world because the celestial powers will be shaken."

This is especially terrifying if we believe current religious teachings that these verses describe something that has never occurred before *and is predicted for our time.*

We tend to view history with detachment because we aren't emotionally connected to those past events. Our personal current experiences, or dread of future experiences, always seem worse because we *feel* the emotion of it.

The fact is, there simply is no catastrophic event new to our earth. Solomon said, "The thing that has been, is what will be again, and that which has been done, is that which will be done again. There is nothing new under the sun. Is there a thing of which it may be said, 'See, this is new?' It has already been, in the vast ages of time—recorded or unrecorded—which were before us" (Ecclesiastes 1:9–10, AMP).

Times have been troubled since sin entered the world. Jesus lived and taught in troubled times. We live and learn from Him in troubled times. Reading Scripture *in its entirety and in context* is critically important to understanding and responding correctly to what we read. The rest of Jesus's statement reassures us "they will see the Son of Man coming ... with power and great glory. *But when these things begin to take place, stand up and lift up your heads, because your redemption is near!*" (Luke 21:27, HCSB).

God is the only constant in a tumultuous world. Jesus said, "I have told you these things, so that *in Me* you may have perfect peace ... in the world you have tribulation, trials, distress and frustration ... take courage! Be confident ... undaunted! I have overcome the world ... I have conquered it for you" (John 16:33, AMP).

Why is it so important to learn about the context of the Scripture you're reading and reading the entirety of the passage rather than scattered verses or chapters?

_____

_____

_____

Think of an example of something you've unknowingly read out of context that created confusion and anxiety.

_____

_____

_____

Write and memorize Ecclesiastes 1:9–10.

_____

_____

_____

_____

Write and memorize John 16:33 (AMP).

_____

_____

_____

The Birth of Jesus and the End of Time

Dr. Dixie, I get irritated every time I hear "peace on earth, goodwill to all men" during the Christmas season. If that's what Jesus came to do, it appears He was a miserable failure. I keep hearing that He's coming soon. So do we just have to live without peace until we die or He shows up?

—Tired of Turmoil

Dear Tired,

When we misquote what the Bible tells us *through the grid of our circumstances* or if we try to lock God's plan into our own emotion-driven understanding of end times, it will always seem like God has failed in some way. What the angels actually said on the night of Jesus's birth was "Glory to God in the highest, and on earth peace among men with whom He is pleased" (Luke 2:14, NASU). This is a promise of peace to those who love God, not a general promise of peace to all men.

Here is an example: We read that Jesus's disciples asked Him how they would know the "end of the age" was near. Jesus listed many things, including wars, earthquakes, false teachers, and famines. We read this through the unrest in the world and the numerous earthquakes in Oklahoma and think Jesus "simply has to" come back tomorrow. But have earthquakes really increased overall?

"As more and more seismographs are installed in the world, more earthquakes can be and have been located. However, the number of large earthquakes, magnitude 6.0 and greater, have stayed relatively constant" (http://earthquake.usgs.gov/earthquakes/eqarchives/year/info_1990s.php).

Jesus clearly said, "You will hear of wars and rumors of wars; *see that you are not frightened or troubled, for this must take place, but the end is not yet*" (Matthew 24:6, AMP).

The world has been troubled and broken from the moment sin entered. Jesus and His disciples lived in troubled times. We live in troubled times. Our modern real-time coverage gives immediate knowledge of both major and minor events all over the world. Around-the-clock coverage of breaking news repeats the story about one murder twenty times, and our minds hear it as twenty murders. Storm chasers repeatedly magnify the possibility and dangers of tornadoes hours before one ever develops so that it seems as though every tornado lasts for hours and hours.

As the angels announced Jesus's birth to the shepherds, the peace they sang about was promised to *men of goodwill, with whom God is pleased* (Luke 2:14, AMP). God is pleased with all who believe in Jesus and receive His life. We have peace because of His life, even in a world filled with turmoil.

Our earth is riddled with sin, broken and trashed by the impact of disobedience to God. In agreement with

God the Father, Jesus humbled Himself to be born fully human and to live His earthly life fully human. First Adam gave the entire human race over to sin; Jesus, last Adam, born of a virgin, redeemed the entire human race from sin. We who have received that gift of redemption are to share this incredible gift with those who haven't received it yet!

The last days of the earth began with the birth of Jesus. The old world systems, the damaged, sin-contaminated ways of thinking and acting, were judged and condemned by His perfect earthly life and His complete and finished victory over sin, Satan, and the world system on the cross. His complete victory was punctuated and declared when He burst from the tomb, fully alive. His ascension to the throne of the universe was the exclamation point.

Are we living in the last days? Let's shout triumphantly with Jesus—*yes!* We live in the last days of sin and wickedness. "And they will see the Son of Man coming ... with power and great glory. *But when these things begin to take place, stand up and lift up your heads, because your redemption is near!*" (Luke 21:27, HCSB).

Who is promised peace? How do we receive that peace?

___

Does receiving the peace of God mean that turmoil and anxiety will be gone? Why or why not?

___

Is it possible to experience peace even when we are emotionally anxious or distraught? Why or why not?

___

Write and memorize John 14:27 (AMP).

___

Christmas Receiving

Dr. Dixie, as usual, I'm not ready for Christmas. Every year I'm more frustrated by the "homey" commercials that seem so fake and the pressure from advertisers to outdo last year with the newest toys, jewelry, and cars. I asked a friend what he thought Jesus would think of the commercialism surrounding His birthday. He just laughed and said, "He'd think it's great. After all, His first miracle was making wine to keep the party going." That seemed pretty shallow to me.

—Grinch

Dear Grinch,

For givers to experience the joy of giving at Christmas, obviously there must be receivers! Gift giving is traditional at this time of the year. The growing commercialism is unavoidable in a culture built on escalation. The gross national product has to increase for the economy to keep growing, people have to buy more for the GNP to increase, and people have to be convinced to buy more; hence, the commercialization of Christmas, Halloween, Easter, Mother's Day, AD infinitum.

Understanding the *why* of Christmas gift giving—that it's the *annual celebration marking and honoring the birth of Jesus of Nazareth*—helps us keep both our spending and our attitudes in balance.

Our Christian Bible is the account of a living gift who was given to pay a debt of sin incurred by humankind—a debt that could not otherwise be paid. Jesus is that gift. He came freely and willingly, given to us from Father God's tender heart of loving-kindness and mercy. Your friend is correct in thinking that Jesus delights in joyful, even hilarious, giving. However, because the reason for giving Christmas gifts has become blurred in our "give me" world, attention is centered more on material things than on the original gift. I often wonder how many families remember to sing "Happy Birthday, dear Jesus" at His own party!

Jesus sacrificed His life to give us the gift of Himself. Sacrifice is inherent in joyful, generous gift giving. Many carefully save money in order to purchase gifts for loved ones. Even when money is plentiful, there is the sacrifice of time to find just the right thing for each person. The sacrifice is repaid in the joy of seeing someone's face light up as the paper is pulled away from the gift. Jesus longs for us to delight in the gift He gave us—Himself.

Whether the centuries-old foundation of Christmas is acknowledged or not, the reality is that when we joyfully give gifts to each other, we commemorate the valuable gifts brought to the baby Jesus by the wise men:

- Gold: a valuable metal signifying that Jesus is King.
- Frankincense: this sweet-smelling resin produces white smoke when burned, symbolizing prayers ascending to heaven. This

gift also symbolizes the sacrifice of Jesus and His priestly role.

- Myrrh: an aromatic herb that is used medicinally to treat severe joint and muscle pain. This gift symbolizes human frailty being healed and restored by the Great Physician.

Jesus being born fully human, living a fully human but sinless life, and Jesus Christ going to the cross, fully human, in order to restore to humanity everything that sin destroyed. Remembering this gift restores enthusiasm to our celebration.

> And after He had appeared in human form ... He carried His obedience to the extreme of death on the cross! Therefore, God has ... freely bestowed on Him the Name that is above every name, that at the Name of Jesus, every knee must bow, in heaven and on earth and under the earth.
>
> Philippians 2:8–11

Why do we celebrate giving at Christmas time?

Do you intentionally highlight the birth of Jesus in your celebration? Why or why not?

What is your understanding of why Jesus came to earth as a human baby?

What did the gifts of gold, frankincense, and myrrh symbolize?

Write and memorize Acts 20:35.

Atheism Says, "Jesus Is Not the Reason"

Dr. Dixie, you probably won't use this because it's long. It may surprise you to know that not everyone is as excited about Jesus as you are. I'm an atheist, and Jesus *isn't* the reason for the season for me. This seems to be true for most Americans since contemporary Christmas is so secularized that it's difficult to find Christian elements. It's more about Santa Claus and commercial profit.

God isn't necessary for us to celebrate the holidays. Some people are so religious they see no point to the holidays without religion. But there are millions of non-Christians who happily celebrate the whole Christmas season without ever acknowledging Christianity.

I am offended by the slogan "Jesus is the reason for the season" because you Christians are obviously attempting to claim ownership of the entire holiday season, not just Christmas day.

Midwinter holidays, however, would continue in the absence of a Christ. Christmas is a mixture of ancient paganism and more-recent Christian traditions such as trees, cards, presents, and mistletoe. These have little or nothing to do with Jesus and his assumed virgin birth. So when we hear the trite slogans, I often wonder, "How was Christ ever central to Christmas?" I see little place where a Christ could be put back into the mix.

When non-Christians celebrate Christmas, the reason for the season is whatever meaning we invest in the holiday—and that's up to us, not to Christians. Simply stated, Christians who insist that Jesus is the reason and needs to be put back into the season are seeking to assert cultural superiority over everyone else. It's another attempt to force Christian privilege in a country that has moved on to religious pluralism.

—Non-Religious

Dear Non-Religious,

It's certainly true that when Christians focus on shopping and "give me" in the same way that unbelievers do, it sends the message that *buying and getting* are really the motivation for Christmas. It's also true that the *holiday season* can be enthusiastically celebrated without even a nod toward Jesus. However, celebrating *Christmas Day* as Jesus's birthday helps shift our focus from all the *holiday stuff* to Him. It's a reminder that the entire year is for loving and giving to others the way Jesus did through His virgin conception, birth, life, death, and resurrection.

Our perceptual meaning for life and its celebrations is always determined by our beliefs. This makes relative truth extremely dangerous and faith in absolute truth essential. An atheist looks at nature and sees evolution, while one who believes that God is the origin of all life will see creation and intelligent design. The same nature, viewed from a different perspective, produces a different conclusion.

In the same way, one who does not believe in the existence and activity of God will approach every aspect of life and death from a human-centered perspective. When God does not exist *in your thinking*, humanism is all that remains. A humanistic perspective doesn't change the fact of God's existence; it does change your conclusions and what form your celebrations take. Because I believe that an eternally existent God is fully involved in the lives of human beings, my approach to the same celebrations are God-centered and have an entirely different emphasis.

It makes perfect sense for you, as an atheist, to say that Christmas can exist without God since from your perspective, *everything exists without God*. However, a Christian perspective says that *nothing can exist without God; therefore, all of life, not just Christmas, is a celebration of the existence of God*. Christmas is the specific celebration of Jesus making God visible to our world through His Incarnation. *Your choosing not to join the celebration doesn't change the basis of the celebration.*

> And she gave birth to her Son, her Firstborn; and she wrapped Him in swaddling clothes and laid Him in a manger ... the angel said to the shepherds, "Do not be afraid; listen! I bring you good news of great joy ... for to you is born this day in the town of David a Savior, Who is Christ the Lord!"
>
> Luke 2

In the middle of the shopping, family gatherings, and giving and receiving of gifts, let's choose to find some quiet moments to receive and be thankful for the greatest gift ever given.

Why does it make sense to an atheist that Christmas can exist completely apart from God?

How would you explain to someone who doesn't believe that Jesus is God, who became human, why you celebrate His birthday? (Hint: avoid using "Christianeze" phrases that an unbeliever wouldn't understand.)

Do you think perception is as important to our conclusion about the existence of God as the evidence we are considering? Why or why not?

What did the gifts of gold, frankincense, and myrrh symbolize?

Write and memorize Acts 20:35.

Jesus: The Reason We Celebrate

Dr. Dixie, I get so frustrated with feeling harassed about celebrating the birth of Jesus at Christmastime. It's not like Christians are forcing others to participate in worshipping Jesus. If anything, it seems like we have come to a place of fully participating in the world's "what can I get" mind-set while minimizing Christ's birth. I know the controversy is more about the public aspect—of visible manger scenes and that sort of thing—but I'm not forcing everyone to take the very public, vulgar, and disgusting billboards and advertisements down even though I find many of them to be very offensive. Why the big issue?

—Glad to Be Christian

Dear Christian,

When Jesus walked on earth, He made an important statement that Christians read, but we often minimize what He meant. He said,

> If the world hates you, understand that it hated Me before it hated you. If you were of the world, the world would love *you as its own*. However, because you are not of the world, but I have chosen you out of it, the world hates you. Remember the word I spoke to you: "A slave is

not greater than his master." If they persecuted Me, they will also persecute you.

John 15:18–20 (HCSB)

It's interesting to notice to whom a *disrespectful attitude* is directed. One doesn't hear "OMB" (Oh my Buddah) or "OMM" (Oh my Mohammad). *Jesus Christ* is a common curse word in our culture, but I've never heard anyone use Hari Krishna's name in vain! It would appear that Satan doesn't bother to attack or encourage disrespect toward a person or system that poses no threat to his agenda of destroying the human race through separation from the one true and living God.

Traditional history tells us that the Apostle Peter requested to be crucified head down because he didn't count himself worthy to die just like Jesus did. All of the apostles and many early believers considered it to be a great honor to die for the name of Jesus.

Understanding the great honor of being treated just like Jesus is essential to keeping us from becoming bitter and resentful toward those who don't understand or respect Christianity. Persecution from the world and from religious systems is simply affirmation of which name is "the real thing."

> She gave birth to her firstborn Son; she wrapped Him snugly in cloth and laid Him in a feeding trough—because there was no room for them at the inn ... there were shepherds in the fields and keeping watch at night over their flock. Then an angel of the Lord stood before them ... and they were terrified. But the angel said to them, "Don't be afraid, for look,

> I proclaim to you good news of great joy that will be for all the people: today a Savior, who is Messiah the Lord, was born for you in the city of David ... Suddenly there was a multitude of the heavenly host with the angel, praising God and saying: Glory to God in the highest heaven, and peace on earth to people He favors!
>
> Luke 2:7–14 (HCSB)

In the middle of the family gatherings and the giving and receiving of gifts, let's each find some quiet moments to receive and be thankful for the greatest gift ever given. As we "open" this priceless gift of salvation, we immediately receive:

- new life
- complete cleansing from sin.

As we continue to "unwrap" the gift through a lifetime of learning and growing in our relationship with Jesus, we receive:

- power to be live victoriously on a sin-contaminated planet
- abundant hope to distribute to a hopeless terror-filled world
- boldness to share our gift with others
- the confident expectation of living forever with Jesus when this life is finished

We continue to honor this beautiful celebration by keeping our focus and emphasis on what the Christmas season is really about—the giving, receiving, and sharing of the gift who never stops giving!

What is the first thing you think of when Christmas is mentioned or the season approaches?

_____
_____
_____

What is your understanding of why we exchange gifts?

_____
_____
_____

In what painful way have you been treated like Jesus? Did you consider it an honor? Why or why not?

_____
_____
_____

How do we "unwrap" the gift of salvation after we've received it?

_____
_____
_____

Read Luke 2:7–14 daily during the Christmas season. To whom is peace promised in verse 14? How do we experience this peace?

_____
_____
_____
_____

New Year's Resolutions

Dr. Dixie, why don't New Year's resolutions last? I'm always so determined until about the middle of February, when I fail and quickly give up. I know other people struggle with this as well. How can I have a different outcome this year?

—Resolved

Dear Resolved,

We might ask if it's impossible to keep our resolutions, why bother to even try to lose weight, manage our money wisely, stop smoking or drinking, exercise more, or spend more time with family? These are the top five resolutions made at the beginning of each New Year.

A new mindset and change in focus will help you succeed. If you begin the New Year believing you're going to fail, you will. If you focus on the long-term benefits and sense of accomplishment, you'll succeed more often than you fail over the course of the year.

Through salvation, Jesus guarantees never-ending life that begins *at the moment we are born into His family*. That means *it is the same life,* whether we are living life on earth in our sin-damaged bodies or with Him in our renewed bodies cleansed from all sin. I will be *me* throughout eternity. You will be *you*. This continuity means that what we do with our time, resources, body, mind, and relationships in our earthly life will radically affect where we "start" in our heavenly life.

Most resolutions don't last past January 31. Failure happens because what we really mean is "I'm beginning a *new month's resolution.*" The very phrase "New Year's resolution" indicates effort lasting at least the next 365 days. Our rapid discouragement reveals that we really believe "it" should happen within the next thirty days or less.

We fail because we expect something inherently "magical" to happen in the "fresh start" of a New Year. The truth is, *January 1 is simply the next day in our everlasting life.* Successful change has to be chosen each day, whether we start in January or July. Resolutions may be set in one day but are accomplished through thousands of choices and tiny steps that happen throughout the following days and months. New Year's resolutions are nothing more than a starting point for establishing new habits that produce lifelong changes.

We often fail because our motivation for change is wrong. If a resolution is based only on dissatisfaction with our personal life experience, if our evaluation is done predominately from a *self*-perspective, with the intention of *self*-improvement based on *self*-discipline, we are doomed to failure from the beginning. If *self-help* could ever be enough to change us, then Jesus did not need to come to earth to live, die, and rise again to empower us to change.

As we choose a plan for change, our evaluation might include these questions:

- Why do I want to read the Bible every day?
- Is it to honor God and grow spiritually?
- Is it because I think it's a good activity to impress God and other people?
- Is my reason for losing weight, exercising more, or eating healthier simply so that others will admire me more?
- Is it to honor God in my body, God's eternal dwelling place? (1 Corinthians 6:19–20)

As we ask God for wisdom about what changes He would have us pursue and how He wants us to work toward them, His power enables us to carry out the decisions that honor Him and are in agreement in His Word (James 1:5).

Jesus declares, "I am the Vine; you are the branches. Whoever remains in Me and I in him, will bear much fruit. Apart from Me, you can do nothing" (John 15:5). With Paul we can confidently say, "I can do everything through Christ Who pours His strength into me" (Philippians 4:13).

Do you make New Year's resolutions? Why or why not?

_____
_____
_____

Do resolutions make a difference in your life? Why or why not?

_____
_____
_____

What changes do you plan to make in your motivation? (Be very specific.)

_____
_____
_____

Write and memorize James 1:5.

_____
_____
_____